Canadian Urban Studies

MONTREAL INSIDE OUT:
A NEW VIEW OF THE CITY

D0925754

Montreal
Inside Out

A NEW VIEW OF THE CITY

John Sobol

ECW PRESS

CANADIAN CATALOGUING IN PUBLICATION DATA

Sobol, John, 1963–

Montreal inside out

Includes bibliographical references.

ISBN 1–55022–159–0

1. Montreal (Quebec) 1. Title.

FC2947.18.S63 1992   917.14'28044   C92–094223–7
FI054.5.M83S63 1992

This book has been published with the assistance of the
Ministry of Culture and Communications of the Province
of Ontario, through funds provided by the Ontario
Publishing Centre, and with the assistance of grants from
the Department of Communications, The Canada Council,
the Ontario Arts Council, and the Government of Canada
through the Canadian Studies and Special Projects Directorate
of the Department of the Secretary of State of Canada.

Design and imaging by ECW Type & Art, Oakville, Ontario.
Printed by Imprimerie Gagné, Louiseville, Québec.

Distributed by General Publishing Co. Limited
30 Lesmill Road, Toronto, Ontario M3B 2T6

Published by ECW PRESS,
1980 Queen Street East, 2nd Floor, Toronto, Ontario M4L 1J2

TABLE OF CONTENTS

List of Illustrations 6

Acknowledgements 7

Introduction 9

Chronology 10

1. History 13

2. Geography and Climate 23

3. Industry and Transportation 31

4. Trade and Commerce 42

5. Neighbourhoods 52

6. Education 62

7. Culture and Lifestyle 71

8. Landmarks and Special Places 86

Suggested Further Reading 99

LIST OF ILLUSTRATIONS

1. The Old Port and downtown 17
2. Calèches at Place D'Armes, December 1989 ... 18
3. Place Jacques Cartier and City Hall in Old Montreal 19
4. The cross on Mount Royal at night 25
5. Plans for improvements to the Lachine Canal .. 34
6. Berri-UQAM Metro Station features modern art . 40
7. Sun Life Building at the corner of Peel and René Lévesque Boulevard 43
8. Houses on Coursol Street in Saint-Henri 54
9. Summer sidewalk sale on Saint-Laurent between Prince Arthur and Pine Avenue 58
10. McGill University's lower campus as seen from Sherbrooke Street 67
11. University of Montreal: aerial view of the main pavilion 69
12. Crowds at Montreal's International Jazz Festival 74
13. The Cirque du Soleil in action: the Baroques 79
14. Maison de la Culture du Plateau Mont-Royal .. 80
15. Snow-covered benches atop Mount-Royal 87
16. Canadian Centre for Architecture and the restored Shaughnessy House 89
17. The Olympic Stadium as seen from Mont-Royal Avenue 91
18. St. Joseph's Oratory 95
19. Cafés on St. Denis 96

ACKNOWLEDGEMENTS

A number of people helped with this book. Thanks are due to Jean-Pierre Paquin and his staff for giving us access to the City of Montreal's photo archives; to Michel Bazinet at Vues D'Ici for being so generous with his photographs of Montreal; to Maurice Boucher at the Canadian Centre for Architecture for showing us photographs from the Centre's collection of Montreal buildings; to Louise Genest at the Montreal International Jazz Festival for providing us with some excellent photographs of the jazz Festival; to Nathalie Belanger at the Cirque du Soleil for providing us with photographs from their collection; to Michel Degray at Juste Pour Voir for generously allowing us to reproduce his and Rejean Beauchamp's photographs; to Monique Denis at Superstock for her cooperation and for giving us permission to reproduce Kurt Scholtz's photograph; to Judy Boundy for her help in finding material for us; to Jocelyn Archambault at the Ministère des Communautés culturelles et de l'immigration for kindly allowing us to reproduce Ronald Maisonneuve's photograph from the Ministère's Calendrier des fêtes des communautés culturelles, 1992; to Erika Watters for her assistance in securing photograph permissions; to Renée Hulan, for her research and guideline preparation; and to Mary Williams, for her detailed copy-editing.

PHOTOGRAPHS: (1) photograph by Michel Degray and Rejean Beauchamp, reproduced by permission of Juste Pour Voir; (2) photograph by Michel Bazinet, reproduced by permission of Vues D'Ici; (3) photograph by Perry Mastrovito, reproduced by permission of Reflexion Photothèques; (4) reproduced by permission of COMSTOCK/R. and B. Kroll; (5) reproduced by permission of the Montreal Archives; (6) photograph by Kurt Scholtz, reproduced by permission of Superstock; (7) reproduced by permission of the Montreal Archives; (8) photograph by Ronald Maisonneuve, reproduced by permission of La Ministère des Communautés culturelles et de l'immigration, gouvernement du Québec; (9) reproduced by permission of the Montreal Archives; (10) photograph by T. Bognar, reproduced by permission of Reflexion Photothèques; (11) reproduced by permission of the Canadian Centre for Architecture; (12) photograph by Denis Alix, reproduced by permission of the Festival International de Jazz; (13) photograph by Dan Lavoie, reproduced by permission of Cirque du Soleil; (14) reproduced by permission of the Montreal Archives; (15) photograph by Michel Bazinet, reproduced by permission of Vues D'Ici; (16) photograph by Geoffrey James, reproduced by permission of the Canadian Centre for Architecture; (17) photograph by Michel Degray and Rejean Beauchamp, reproduced by permission of Juste Pour Voir; (18) photograph by Perry Mastrovito, reproduced by permission of Reflexion Photothèques; (19) reproduced by permission of COMSTOCK/George Hunter.

INTRODUCTION

All cities are unique; but, to borrow a phrase, some are more unique than others. In its uniqueness, Montreal arguably rivals New Orleans and Kathmandu. Why? Mostly because — and this is a crucial fact that very few people unfamiliar with the city truly understand — Montreal, in the province of Quebec, is a French city in North America: people speak French in the streets, in their homes, on television, in shops. Of course, there are anglophones in Montreal, as well as Portuguese, Greek, Italian, Hebrew, and Hindi speakers, among many others, but without minimizing the importance of these groups to the urban fabric, it is Montreal's francophones — their language and their culture — that make Montreal such an unusual and intriguing metropolis.

Montreal, an island in the St. Lawrence River, is an emotional city. To walk its streets is to sense a mood — sometimes warm, sometimes anxious, depending upon the political climate — but always invigorating and vital. The Québécois culture offers a striking contrast to that of the rest of North America. Montreal is far more European, epicurean, and stylish than most — or perhaps any other — North American city.

This book won't be able to recreate the genuine Montreal experience; to feel that special aura you'll have to visit the city yourself. But it will offer a glimpse into the lives and attitudes of Montrealers, the beauty and rough charm of the city, and the rich historical legacy that informs its everyday life.

Montreal celebrated its 350th anniversary in 1992. Festivities of all kinds were scheduled throughout the summer everywhere on the island of Montreal. But, as you'll see, even daily life in the city — if not exactly a constant celebration — is a constant stream of stimulating sights, sounds, tastes, events, and people. It is a city that, once visited, is impossible to forget.

9

Pre-1535   Hochelaga, an Iroquois village with a population of approximately 1,500, has been in existence for an indeterminate period on the site of what is to become Montreal.

1535   The first European explorer, Jacques Cartier, arrives at Hochelaga.

1543   Cartier visits the village a second time.

1603   Sixty years elapse before the arrival of the next European, Samuel de Champlain. He finds that the village of Hochelaga has long been abandoned. The fate of the original Iroquois inhabitants is unknown.

1642   Montreal's founder, Paul de Chomedey, Sieur de Maisonneuve, arrives at the site of Hochelaga accompanied by about fifty people, four of whom are women. Construction begins on Ville Marie, a mission supported by the Societé-de-Nôtre-Dame-de-Montréal.

1663   The seminary of St. Sulpice is given seigneurial rights over the island of Montreal, which they will retain for nearly two centuries.

1701   A peace treaty between the Iroquois and the French assures the colony's survival.

1660–1759 The fur trade grows rapidly, and Montreal becomes the hub of the traders' (called *coureurs de bois*) extensive network. The explorers La Salle, La Vérendrye, and d'Iberville are all based in the community that is becoming known as Montreal.

1760   A year after the defeat of French Major-General Montcalm and his troops on the Plains of Abraham at Quebec City, Montreal surrenders to the British forces. The British conquest has little economic effect. The fur trade remains the colony's primary resource.

1789   The population of Montreal reaches 5,500.

1815   The influx of British settlers leads to a population boom. By 1825, Montreal has 22,540 residents, and nearly double that only 20 years later.

1817   The Bank of Montreal is founded.

1832   The City of Montreal is incorporated. Jacques Viger, one of 16 councillors for 8 *quartiers*, is elected mayor.

1837   Louis-Joseph Papineau leads the Patriote rebellions against the British, but is defeated in a military skirmish. Papineau escapes to the United States.

1844–49   Montreal is briefly named capital of British North America. After rioters burn down the Parliament Buildings, Toronto is chosen as a replacement.

1856   The Grand Trunk Railway of Canada opens a line between Montreal and Toronto. Three years later, another is opened that links Montreal and Quebec City.

1859   The Victoria Bridge, which traverses the St. Lawrence River, joining the island of Montreal and the river's south shore, is completed.

1874   Mount Royal Park is created.

1891   Montreal's population reaches 216,650.

1905–18   The Municipality of Montreal annexes 20 smaller communities on the island of Montreal.

1934   Montreal's population of over one million has been impoverished by the Great Depression. The city can no longer afford to meet its debts, and is placed under trusteeship.

1945–59   World War II helps stimulate the economy, which rebounds and grows dramatically. An influx of predominantly European immigrants accelerates Montreal's already rapid growth. Maurice Duplessis, the provincial premier who has for eighteen years maintained a rigid, highly conservative control over Quebec's affairs, dies in office in 1959. In the same year, the St. Lawrence Seaway opens.

1960   Jean Lesage is elected premier of the province of Quebec. The Quiet Revolution begins.

1967   Montreal hosts the World's Fair — Expo 67.

1976   Montreal hosts the Summer Olympics. They are a success as an athletic event, but run up a deficit of two billion dollars for the city and its unhappy taxpayers.

1986   After nearly 30 years as mayor of Montreal, Jean Drapeau steps down. His Civic Party is crushed in the next election, and Jean Doré, head of the Montreal's Citizen's Movement, becomes Montreal's forty-eighth mayor.

1992   Montreal celebrates its 350th birthday.

I

HISTORY

TO LIVE IN MONTREAL is to live as close to history as one possibly can in a North American city. Despite what took place in the dark years of the 1960s and 1970s — Montreal's urban planners replaced many old buildings and neighbourhoods with efficient, modern, yet faceless new ones — much of the city's architectural heritage remains intact.

Strolling through Old Montreal, an area of two square kilometres bounded to the south by the city's port, one is instantly transported to another era. For it was here that the settlement of Ville Marie was founded some 350 years ago. Entire city blocks of stone buildings from earlier centuries have been preserved in Old Montreal, as have cobblestone streets and small sections of the city's original walls. A few homes scattered about the Montreal area date back more than 300 years, and are among the oldest in North America.

Montrealers are tied to their history not only by the buildings that speak of a bygone age, but also by the city's vibrant French-Canadian, or Québécois culture. The Québécois language and culture permeate the life of the city, and stand out in sharp relief against a continent dominated by the English language and by American culture. For all Montrealers, whether they be francophone, anglophone, Native, or allophone, the uniqueness of Montreal life, and consequently the importance of history, can never be forgotten.

Montreal was founded at a time when the Iroquois Confederacy of Nations controlled the St. Lawrence River region. Although the village of Hochelaga (Place of the Beaver Dams) had disappeared a half-century earlier, the island was still crisscrossed with paths used by Native hunters and trappers.

Some historians and many Natives believe that the village vanished as a result of diseases brought by Jacques Cartier on his visits in 1535 and 1543. Cartier was the first European explorer to come to Hochelaga. Others attribute its disappearance to war, famine, or simply to the nomadic nature of its inhabitants. It seems unlikely we will ever know the truth.

In the mid-seventeenth century, France was in the grips of an anti-Reformation religious fervour, and after lobbying tenaciously, the Association-de-Nôtre-Dame-Pour-la-Conversion-des-Sauvages-de-la-Nouvelle-France-en-L'île-de-Montréal was given proprietary rights over the island in 1642. That name in English is the Association of Nôtre Dame for the Conversion of the Savages on the Island of Montreal in New France. Today we understand that "converting" actually means destroying the Native people's way of life and heritage, but, at that time, European Catholics were convinced that their way was the only way. The association paid sixty thousand French *livres* to the Sieur de Maisonneuve, founder of the settlement of Ville Marie (later Montreal), to cover the expenses of mounting an expedition with the goal of saving the souls of the St. Lawrence Iroquois. But the conquests of these zealous missionaries would be few. Although a small group of Iroquois were successfully "converted," many more resisted the imposition of a new religion by the white settlers. Native people already had their own religion and culture, which was based on respect for their land and ancestors. The association's missionary aim, therefore, was eventually supplanted by a more material one: to develop the colony as a trading centre.

The first decades of settlement were marked by tremendous hardship for the French adventurers who crossed the Atlantic. The fierce winters and the Iroquois' violent resistance to their presence took many lives. But as the demand for fur grew in Europe, the possibility of making a small fortune in the fur trade outweighed the potential risk, and many intrepid young Frenchmen poured into the colony. Further down the St. Lawrence River, north of Quebec city, farmers were being given plots of land along the water's edge. These long narrow strips of land, known as *rangs*, were distributed according to the neo-feudal seigneurial system. But it would be several generations before farming would become an important part of Montreal's development. Fur remained the primary focus in Montreal.

The government of New France, as the colony was known, was assigned in 1627 to La Compagnie des Cents Associés. La Compagnie was a commercial organization created by the famous French minister Cardinal Richelieu. In exchange for the responsibility of administering the colony, La Compagnie was to have exclusive trapping rights throughout its vast area. But while the fur trade profited nicely during the next three decades, the administration of the colony was not a success. In 1663, after the colony had suffered 10 years of Iroquois raids and seen its population dwindle, Louis XIV officially registered New France as a French province, sent troops to defend it, and established a more responsible system of government.

The French king created two administrative posts, and invested those who filled them with the authority to run the province in a similar fashion to France itself. The governor of the colony was responsible for military matters and foreign affairs, while the intendant oversaw the administration of justice, finances, and the exigencies of everyday civil life.

But despite the grand titles of New France's administrators, and in some cases their remarkable achievements, the tiny settlement of Ville Marie struggled to survive. Fluctuations in the fur market had a direct and sometimes drastic effect on the lives of early Montrealers, to say nothing of disease and the harsh elements. In the early years of the eighteenth century, a fortified wall was built around the village to fend off attacks by Natives. But these rudimentary palisades were of little use when it came to war, and when Montreal was held under siege by the British in 1760, surrender was all but inevitable.

After the British conquest, Montreal's influence as a fur-trading centre continued to grow. The Montreal-based North West Company was engaged in a fierce rivalry with the Hudson's Bay Company. Unlike the Hudson's Bay Company traders, who waited for furs to be brought to their outposts along the shores of Hudson Bay, the North West Company's traders, known as *coureurs de bois*, travelled deep into the interior of the continent to seek out trading partners. Although their aims were commercial, on their expeditions these *coureurs de bois* mapped out the enormous breadth of a continent previously unexplored by Europeans. Their names feature prominently in history books not as traders, but as the first white explorers of the Mississippi, the Rockies, and the Plains of the Midwest.

Since its founding, there had been very few women in New France, and fewer still in Montreal — at least, very few European women. A single wedding per year was the norm for the first few decades of Montreal's existence. Not surprisingly, many Frenchmen insisted on taking Native wives, which likely fuelled the constant antagonism between Natives and whites. No record exists that explains how Native women felt about these marriages, but we do know that such unions were deplored by the still-influential clergy in New France. In 1663, Louis XIV ordered eight hundred women, many of them beggars, prostitutes, or simply poor women with little power over their own destinies, to be shipped to New France to be married. *Les filles du roi*, as these young women are known to history, had little idea of what awaited them. But despite the fear and hardship they experienced, they gave birth to a generation of children whose descendants can be found in every corner of modern Quebec.

Montreal was officially incorporated in 1832. Within three decades, the city's economic base had shifted away from the fur trade; Montreal had become an international port and manufacturing centre. The construction at Trois Rivières (about 150 kilometres down the St. Lawrence River) of the first North American steamship, *The Accommodation*, signalled the dawning of the industrial era in Montreal. Much of the industrial activity was related to the shipping industry, and Montreal's port, which had always been the city's lifeline, has remained a vital element in its modern economy. The completion, in 1958, of the St. Lawrence Seaway, a vast network of locks and canals that permits oceangoing vessels to travel throughout the Great Lakes-St. Lawrence hydrographic region, assured the continuing importance of Montreal's shipping industry and port.

The city grew up around the port, and photographs from the mid-nineteenth century show how remarkably unchanged parts of it remain today. Although cars now outnumber horse-

FIGURE I

The Old Port and downtown

FIGURE 2

Calèches at Place D'Armes, December 1989

FIGURE 3

Place Jacques Cartier and City Hall in Old Montreal

drawn buggies, *calèches* filled with tourists still trot about Old Montreal and along the riverfront. On a misty winter night, after an evening spent in one of Old Montreal's many restaurants or bistros, stepping out into lamplit and cobblestoned St. Paul Street is like stepping into an earlier era.

Old Montreal is not only one of Montreal's most popular tourist areas, it is also an important cultural reference point, especially for French Montrealers. City Hall is located at the northern edge of Place Jacques Cartier, the heart of the old city, and it was in 1967, from a balcony of that building, that French president General Charles de Gaulle gave a legendary speech. He spoke the words "vive le Québec libre," echoing the slogan of Québécois nationalists, and stirring up passionate feelings across the country. He later claimed that he hadn't realized the implications of his words, but no retraction could alter the effects of his public endorsement of Quebec sovereignty.

By 1861, Montreal's population had grown to 108,000, swollen by an influx of rural Quebecers. This plentiful supply of labour, along with the construction of the Lachine Canal (skirting the Lachine Rapids at the southern tip of the island, and allowing the passage of goods further upriver) in 1825, and the inauguration of the Grand Trunk Railway in 1856, spurred further advances in industry. Foundries, factories, machine shops, and mills were established to the west of the port, many of them alongside the Lachine Canal, where they could make use of its hydraulic capacity. This area remains a small industrial centre today, but dramatic job losses have been suffered there in the wake of a general exodus of industries towards suburban industrial parks.

Montreal's greatest public park, Mount Royal, was officially given its status in 1875. "The mountain," as it is universally known to Montrealers, is an old volcanic hill whose rounded peak reaches a height of only about 225 metres. Yet despite its size, the mountain is visible from anywhere on the island. After a stubborn landowner named Lamothe chopped down all the trees on one flank of the mountain in 1860, the city's residents insisted that such insensitive actions be curtailed. Most of the mountain was turned into a spacious natural park. It was ingeniously landscaped by Frederick Law Olmsted, who also designed New York's Central Park and established Yosemite National Park in California.

The early twentieth century was a prosperous era for Montreal. The city's population was booming, still fuelled largely by the constant arrival of young men and women from rural Quebec. There were, however, by this time, other communities — Irish, Scottish, Black — with deep roots in the city. The Irish districts of Griffintown and Victoriaville, along with the neighbouring St. Antoine district, Montreal's first Black neighbourhood, supplied much of the workforce for the nearby railyards. The Irish had been immigrating to North America since the early nineteenth century, and though they were never as numerous in Montreal as they were in eastern Quebec or New England, they played an important role in building Montreal, and Irish names are still quite commonly found as surnames of both anglophone and francophone Quebecers.

The first Black people in New France were slaves. Olivier Le Jeune was sold at auction in Canada as early as 1629, and by 1759 there were approximately one thousand Black slaves in New France. By the time the British courts abolished slavery in 1833, the practice had already been on the decline in Montreal for some decades. When the Grand Trunk and Canadian Pacific railways made Montreal their training and maintenance headquarters in the late nineteenth century, the Black community mushroomed; many American men and their families came north in search of work and better living conditions. By the 1920s, the number of Blacks in Montreal had reached three thousand. The St. Antoine district was a vibrant neighbourhood for much of this century, but it met with economic hardship as the railways moved west, and has been subjected to several terribly misguided urban-planning decisions.

In recent years, Montreal has attracted a large number of francophone Blacks. Many Haitians, for example, have sought refuge from their troubled homeland in Quebec. Italian, Greek, and Portuguese immigrants, along with Eastern European Jews, also established significant communities in Montreal at the turn of this century, which continue to flourish to this day.

Political power in Montreal has traditionally been shared by the official government of the day and the tremendously influential Catholic church. After having slowly consolidated its power during the eighteenth and nineteenth centuries, the church, by the mid-twentieth century, oversaw virtually all educational institutions, labour unions, and many other nominally secular organizations. Not until the Quiet Revolution of the early 1960s did the influence of the church shrink significantly.

Montreal's municipal government underwent many modifications before finally becoming a genuinely democratic institution. In 1940, for example, city council was reformed to ensure the representation of Montreal's élite; one-third of the councillors were elected exclusively by property owners, one-third by property owners and tenants combined, and one-third was appointed by the Chamber of Commerce and other influential groups (the church, for example). This arrangement allowed a few powerful individuals to shape virtually all municipal policies. Remarkably, it was not until 1970 that all city councillors were elected by universal suffrage. Another result of the church's conservative influence was that Quebec's women were not permitted to vote in provincial elections until 1940.

Since 1914, Montreal has had but eight mayors, three of whom (Médéric Martin, Camillien Houde, and Jean Drapeau) served over 60 years between them. It was Jean Drapeau who fought to put Montreal on the international map, succeeding with several grand projets, including Expo 67 (the world's fair) and the 1976 Summer Olympics Games. By 1986, however, Montrealers had grown tired of Drapeau's Civic Party and its autocratic and expensive regime. They turned to the long-suffering Montreal Citizen's Movement, which was elected in a landslide — the Civic Party won only two seats. Jean Doré became Montreal's second mayor in 30 years.

2

GEOGRAPHY AND CLIMATE

WHAT DO MONTREAL, Manhattan, and Singapore have in common? The answer, of course, is that they are all island cities. Montreal is one of a handful of important urbanized isles that are strategically located both militarily and economically. Montreal lies in the great St. Lawrence River, sixteen hundred kilometres inland from the Atlantic Ocean, and is ideally placed to regulate marine traffic flowing in or out of the enormous Great Lakes hydrographic system.

Montreal is also one of the largest island cities, which may be why one can still find isolated nooks and crannies on it that retain a trace of their original natural state. Here and there on the island a few small plots of land, mostly oversized backyards now, are still farmed, and may even be home to a chicken or two. But these sanctuaries are few and far between, for most of the island is taken up by the loud and intimidating trappings of a modern metropolis. Skyscrapers and airports, railroads and highways, have claimed the island, to say nothing of the hundreds of thousands of homes, shops, offices, churches, and other buildings. Along all the island's riverbanks but the industrialized southern one are pleasant suburbs, both new and old. These are popular with those who seek a more relaxed way of life a short commute from the city centre.

The island itself is shaped like that ever-popular French pastry, the *croissant*, or crescent. Because of its pronounced curve, Montrealers have for years conveniently, yet mistakenly, identified the city's northern and southern areas as east and west. Sherbrooke Street, which is considered to be Montreal's primary east-west axis, actually runs almost directly north for much of its length. So if you need directions in Montreal, remember to leave your compass at home.

Lengthwise, from tip to tip, the island of Montreal measures approximately 50 kilometres, while at its widest it reaches about 16 kilometres. It has an area of approximately 174 square kilometres. Montreal lies in the centre of the St. Lawrence Lowlands region of the province of Quebec, sandwiched between the Canadian Shield to the north, and the Appalachian region to both the south and east.

Montreal is the largest of the islands that form the Hochelaga Archipelago, at the confluence of the Ottawa and St. Lawrence rivers. The rivers meet just beyond the municipality of Ste. Anne de Bellevue, at the western tip of the island, in a scenic basin known as Lake of Two Mountains. From there, the Rivière des Prairies flows to the north of the island, while the main branch of the mighty St. Lawrence flows to the south. The two rivers rejoin at the eastern tip of the island, just beyond the small community of Pointe aux Trembles.

During Montreal's severe winter, much of the water surrounding the island turns to ice. Even the swift and powerful St. Lawrence is sometimes covered by a sheet of purplish ice that hides the torrent below. Many of the smaller inlets are frozen solid for months at a time, and during those rare winters that bring cold temperatures and little or no snow these extensive natural ice plains attract thousands of skaters on weekends. Ice fishing, too, is a popular winter pastime for many Montrealers, and ice-fishing huts are a common sight on Lake of Two Mountains every winter.

To the north of Montreal, connected by a series of bridges across Rivière des Prairies, lies Île Jésus. Along its northern shore, Île Jésus is divided from the mainland by Rivière des Mille Îles, which also issues from the Lake of Two Mountains, and merges with Rivière des Prairies, and then with the main artery of the St. Lawrence at the eastern tip of the island of Montreal. Île Jésus is more commonly referred to as Laval, which is the name of the largest municipality on the island. Laval is at once a suburb of Montreal, and a self-contained city with a total population of close to 300,000. Laval is far less scenic than Montreal, as it was only in the postwar years that most of its buildings were constructed. Laval, and the neighbouring community of Chomedey, are home to many

FIGURE 4

The cross on Mount Royal at night

immigrant communities, including sizable Italian, Greek, and Jewish ones.

Montreal is, on the whole, a flat, low-lying city. It has one notable geographic feature, however, one that gives the city its name: Mount Royal. Admittedly, at a height of 225 metres, Mount Royal would hardly pass for a mountain in Switzerland, or in the Rockies, but for Montrealers, it's not the mountain's size that matters so much as its place in the city's collective heart. Much of the mountain, which is located more or less at the centre of the island, has been an enormous municipal park for over a century, and the park is a popular site for a great range of outdoor activity year-round.

Despite its grand name, Mount Royal is actually little more than a knoll, one of the Monteregian Hills. These ancient volcanic hills, which include nearby Mount St. Hilaire and Mount St. Bruno, rise up out of the plains between the Laurentian and the Appalachian mountain ranges. Mount Royal is essentially a big block of gabbro, a type of igneous rock, with three equidistant peaks. Two of these peaks, located in the municipalities of Westmount and Outremont, slope gradually for several kilometres. The third and highest peak, the one that most Montrealers call Mount Royal, has such steep cliffs that from the lookout near its peak you can lean right over downtown.

Mount Royal is not the city's only important park. Along the southwestern shore of the island, running through the towns of Verdun, Lachine, and Lasalle, Montreal boasts an extended riverfront park, the Lachine Canal Park. Bicycle paths run for more than 20 kilometres along the canal and the river. Lachine is also the location of the city's main pleasure-boat marina. The Lachine Rapids, which for centuries thwarted attempts to manoeuvre oceangoing vessels past Montreal into the Great Lakes, remains a popular tourist attraction. And while the rapids may not be as ferocious as those in Quebec's northern wilderness, they are able to support a thriving white-water rafting business.

Another vital Montreal park is Maisonneuve Park, home of Montreal's world-class Botanical Garden. The park is situated directly across from the monumental Olympic Stadium, and was established in 1931 by Brother Marie-Victorin, a botanist and a member of the faculty of the University of Montreal. The park is an oasis of green that features an intriguing variety of trees and plants. The Botanical Garden is considered the second most important of its kind in the world, and numbers among its many natural attractions the largest collection of bonsai trees outside of Asia, a Chinese garden based on the mountain and water gardens of the Ming Dynasty, and an insectarium. Montreal's natural flora consists of an abundance of coniferous and deciduous trees. Maple, birch, ash, poplar, oak, pine, and cedar are the most common varieties of trees in the city, although others can be found. Groves of lilacs in bloom can be found in several downtown parks in spring, offering up their exceptional perfume. As they were in most North American cities, Montreal's elm trees were destroyed by Dutch elm disease. Those who wish to lose themselves for an afternoon in a quiet forest setting head for the Morgan Arboretum in Ste. Anne de Bellevue, a short drive from the city. The arboretum, which is administered by McGill University, has four hundred acres of mixed hardwood and softwood forest, and two hundred acres of trees of various species planted in sections. The goal of the arboretum's administrators has been to include as many types of indigenous Canadian trees as possible.

During its first two hundred years, Montreal's existence was circumscribed by the river and the mountain. By the late nineteenth century, the city had expanded to the east, west, and north. Many of the streets that eventually became major thoroughfares started out as carriage trails, or, in some cases (such as that of Côte St. Antoine), as paths established many centuries ago by the island's Native inhabitants.

One of the longest and oldest streets in Montreal is Nôtre Dame Street, a route first blazed by Dollier de Casson in 1660. It runs nearly the entire length of the island's southern shore, through the heart of the city to the eastern tip of the island. Sections of the street are residential, others financial (the stock exchange is on Nôtre Dame). To the east it is lined with many of Montreal's heaviest industries. At night, oil refineries, giant, futuristic structures, light up one stretch of Nôtre Dame. For someone who lives in the residential neighbourhood of St.

Henri, many kilometres to the west, it's hard to believe that the same quaint Nôtre Dame Street on which they shop, do laundry, or go to school, could also be so ugly and impersonal. Unfortunately, the east-end oil refineries are not the only unpleasant sites on the island. Due to the shortsightedness of an earlier generation, Montreal has the Miron Quarry. Astoundingly, this quarry, which is the largest garbage-disposal site and incinerator in the province, is located right in the heart of a dense residential district. City officials have been tightening controls on what kinds of refuse can be burned and buried at the site, but children still play in beautiful Laurier Park beneath the shadow of the quarry's red and white smokestacks. Seen from the air, the quarry is like a deep gash in the middle of the city — it is a legacy of a less environmentally conscious age.

Today Montreal is covered by a vast network of roads, making transportation between distant neighbourhoods easy. But it was not always so. The district of Côte des Neiges, which is now accessible from anywhere in the city by subway, was once a half-day's journey by carriage from the city centre. As the city grew and grew, such once-distant municipalities were absorbed into it, and, in most cases, few traces remain of their village origins.

Montreal's urban landscape is dominated by several types of structures: skyscrapers, churches, and the characteristic triplexes in which a great many Montrealers live. These buildings have a flat on each floor and steep exterior stairways, many of which are curved or spiralled. If Montreal's homes have a single distinctive feature, like the doors of Dublin or the brown stone of New York, it is these vertiginous staircases. Yet while they may be picturesque, some displaying excellent crafting and grillwork, in the deep of winter they can also be extremely perilous. Triplex dwellers compare tales of late-night or early-morning tumbles down Montreal's famous stairs. Most, however, have grown adept at negotiating icy exterior stairs — it is only one of the many challenges of winter life.

Montreal's climate is dominated by winter. Technically, Montreal's winter lasts only five months, from mid-November to mid-April, but the first frost falls in early October, and the last often occurs well into May. During their few precious summer months, Montrealers celebrate the sun and heat with a devotion that matches — perhaps exceeds — that of Californians.

Yet winter is considered a blessing, too, and when the first snow falls on the city, often in the form of a blizzard, its citizens experience a collective thrill. Montrealers are a hardy bunch, and, for the most part, pride themselves on their ability to overcome metre-high snowdrifts — few things can amuse them more than news reports of two inches of snow paralyzing Texas. It is also worth noting that so many Montrealers have migrated to Florida that Montreal newspapers are sold in many Florida newsstands.

City planners have displayed some resourcefulness in finding solutions to the restrictions the long months of snow and cold can impose. Montreal's network of transportation systems, shopping malls, and offices interconnected by subterranean tunnels, referred to in promotional literature (although the term is not generally used by Montrealers) as the Underground City, has made it possible to travel beneath downtown in shirtsleeves for blocks on end, even when the temperature outside is -30° C (-22° F).

How often does it actually get that cold? Well, it depends. The coldest months of the year are January and February, when the average temperature hovers around -10° C (14° F). But averages are misleading, because they may encompass a string of five or six consecutive days at -25° C (-13° F), followed by another week at -5° C (23° F). The coldest temperature on record in Montreal is -37.8° C (-36° F), but if we consider the wind-chill factor, we understand why it's not unusual for it to feel colder than that.

Strangely enough, the hottest temperature recorded in Montreal is also 37.8° C (100° F), this time above zero. Only Moscow, of all the major cities in the world, experiences more dramatic temperature swings than Montreal. Of course, smaller cities, such as the Prairie city of Regina, Saskatchewan, can top even Moscow. (Regina's record high is 43.3° C [110° F], and record low is -50° C [-58° F]!) So by Canadian standards, Montreal's climate is not the harshest after all.

Along with the cold, snow is the other essential ingredient of a Montreal winter. While statistics show that snowfall has gradually decreased over the past two decades, Montreal nonetheless receives more than its share. The average annual accumulation is 232 centimetres (or nearly 8 feet), and sometimes, by the time Montrealers have shovelled the snow from their driveways and outdoor stairways onto already massive drifts, the city begins to resemble a series of trenches dug in a terrain of solid snow. Other years, however, a brief January thaw can melt off most of it in just a day or two.

It is axiomatic to Montrealers that the city never really experiences spring. Winter simply drags into a wet and muddy May, which blossoms, seemingly overnight, into a summery June. Though spring may be denied them, many Montrealers declare the city's gorgeous autumn their favourite season. In late September, when the leaves begin to fall across the city, when Mount Royal starts to turn a deep crimson, and when the heat of the summer has been replaced by the cool, aromatic autumn air, few can resist revelling in the season. Even in the gritty urban environment, the air has a certain freshness.

July and August are the hottest and wettest months of the year in Montreal. The average temperature is 20° C (68° F), but during the day it is usually much hotter. The combination of heat and humidity can be overwhelming, especially at night, when trying to sleep becomes an irritating challenge. Large numbers of Montrealers escape to their cottages in the Laurentian Mountains to the north of the city, but most remain to cope with the rigours of the season. But again, despite its trials, summer is avidly welcomed when it arrives and bitterly lamented when it is gone.

3

INDUSTRY AND TRANSPORTATION

TODAY'S MONTREALER CAN CHOOSE from a mesmerizing array of modes of transport. To cross town one can walk, ride a bicycle, take the subway (known as the Metro), climb on a bus, drive a car or motorcycle, take a taxi, or, in some cases, even take a commuter train. If that same Montrealer has a longer trip to make, two airports are available: Dorval and Mirabel. Of course, this traveller might choose to journey by rail (Montreal is one hub in a vast network of continental rail routes), or by intercity bus. But the one mode of transport a Montrealer will in all likelihood not choose is the one that is responsible for the city's existence: the ship.

Montreal, after all, *is* an island, and could only be reached by ship until the first bridge linking it to the mainland was built in 1859. In a larger sense, too, Montreal's destiny has always been linked to its ability to respond to the demands of maritime industries. Encompassing the early wooden clippers and frigates and the enormous container vessels that dock in the port of Montreal today, the city's economic history is largely a history of taming and exploiting the St. Lawrence River.

In the early days of New France, Montreal's location offered both a valuable advantage and a harmful disadvantage with respect to the small, but vital and ever-growing shipping industry. The advantage, which would benefit the city for over three hundred years, until the opening of the St. Lawrence Seaway in 1959, was that no oceangoing vessel could travel through the treacherous shallows and rapids upstream from the island. This meant that Montreal was the natural point for all cargo shipped between the enormous Great Lakes inland region and anywhere else in the world to be transferred from lake travellers to sea vessels. At first, it was predominantly furs that were trans-shipped at Montreal, but eventually grain, coal, and manu-factured goods would constitute the bulk of the cargo. Montreal's port thus needed a constant supply of manual labourers, and for the first two hundred years of its existence, many Montrealers were employed in some capacity related to the comings and goings of ships.

Montreal's disadvantage was that it was several hundred kilometres upstream from Quebec City, which had established itself early on as the most important port on the St. Lawrence River. Few ships had a reason to continue their journey up-stream to the small outpost that was Montreal, especially since the journey was slow and arduous due to the tricky shoals along the way. In fact, in the early eighteenth century, the trip took so long that even relatively small ships could only make one visit a season. The Eweretta, for example, owned by the most important economic unit of Montreal's early years, the North West Company, would arrive in late spring, after the ice had thawed, loaded with clothing, food, and other valuable items from France. It would leave months later, well into autumn but before the river froze, filled to the brim with beaver pelts. Obviously, if Montreal was to grow into an important city, movement upstream would have to be made easier.

In 1851, after years of lobbying, John Young, the first chairman of the Montreal Harbour Commission, finally convinced the government that money should be spent to dredge the shoals in Lac St. Pierre, downstream from Montreal. When the project was completed in 1857, the shoals had been deepened from a mere 10 feet to 18 feet, and could now accommodate even the largest ocean clipper.

But soon there was a new problem. Steamships were rapidly coming to dominate the shipping industry. Whereas only the heaviest wooden ships weighed more than two thousand tons, the new steamships often weighed four thousand, or more. Again, years of lobbying were required, but, in 1901, a victory was won for Montreal's shipping industry, and for the city as a whole the prime minister of Canada, Sir Wilfrid Laurier, agreed that the channel leading to Montreal should be deepened to 30 feet.

That might sound like the end of this story — but it isn't. There is one more crucial chapter, and that concerns the building of the St. Lawrence Seaway. The first canal along the St. Lawrence River was begun as early as 1783, and, over the next century and a half, many more were built, including the important Lachine Canal, in 1825. By the 1930s, a lively debate had arisen over the value of an entire series of locks and canals that would allow oceangoing ships to travel up the St. Lawrence and through the Great Lakes. In Montreal, many were opposed to the idea, precisely because it threatened the city's privileged position as intermediary between the two shipping systems. It would also cost an enormous sum to accomplish such an engineering feat. But, in the end, the promoters of the plan won the support of the federal government, who, after the end of World War II, saw the development of the seaway as an important strategic defense initiative.

And so the St. Lawrence Seaway was built, in cooperation with the government of the United States. It was completed in 1959, and allowed westbound ships of more than 200 metres in length and drawing 8 metres or less to be lifted nearly 180 metres from their passage through Montreal to their arrival in Thunder Bay at the head of Lake Superior. The ships travelled through an extensive network of locks and canals, many of them, such as the Beauharnois and St. Lambert locks, near Montreal. The result was a four-fold increase in marine traffic on the St. Lawrence in just a few decades, although a far smaller proportion of that traffic now actually stops in the port of Montreal.

The construction of this system of canals may have been harmful to Montreal's transshipping industry, but the digging of the Lachine Canal earlier, in 1823, and the renovation of it in 1848, actually signalled the development of the city as the industrial capital of Canada in the nineteenth century. It was the hydraulic power made available by the canal that fostered the creation of engineering industries, factories, and machine shops of all kinds in the 1840s and 50s. This industrial boom was a crucial stage in the city's economic development, and was accompanied by the establishment of a host of financial institutions, such as banks and insurance companies, to accommodate the elevated flow of capital.

FIGURE 5

Plans for improvements to the Lachine Canal

The mid-nineteenth century was also the era of the great railway expansion in Canada, and it saw the transformation of Montreal's fur-based economy, the last vestiges of it, into a fully integrated modern one. Now the city had a large network of rail routes that could serve the West's ever-growing demand for manufactured goods.

Iron foundries were built along the Lachine Canal, casting engines, machine parts, boilers, cranes, pumps, nails, and many other much-needed products. Other factories used hydraulic power to manufacture paint and textiles, or to saw lumber. But while many of its entrepreneurs were jumping on the industrial bandwagon, it took Montreal a long time to develop an interest in the railway.

While in Britain the development of railways was proceeding at a feverish pitch, in British North America its pace was sluggish. It may be surprising that a mode of transportation that could function year-round — shipping was limited by ice to seven months of the year — would not be embraced by Montreal entrepreneurs. But it was not, and mostly for the simple reason that the river had served them well, and the need to switch to rail simply wasn't felt. Eventually, however, the railway did begin to have an impact.

The first Canadian railway was the Champlain and St. Lawrence, which opened in 1836, and ran from the southern shore of the St. Lawrence River across from Montreal north to St. Jean-sur-Richelieu, on the Richelieu River. Eight years later, a far more ambitious railway was proposed, the St. Lawrence and Atlantic, which would eventually run from Montreal to Portland, Maine. It was built, in part, as a response to the threat of losing western trade to the city of Boston, which had built a train link from Lake Champlain west to Ogdensburg, New York. The St. Lawrence and Atlantic Railway, eventually completed in 1853, gave Montreal, Quebec City, and Sherbrooke easy and efficient access to a year-round ice-free port, and thus represented a major safeguard against Boston's attempt at usurping commercial power.

In the years that followed, many more rail lines were constructed, and many personal fortunes were also built in the unfettered rail market. The Montreal and Lachine Railway was completed in 1847, and would become the first leg of a western railway system. In 1851, Montreal became connected by rail to Boston and New York. And in 1853, the tremendously important Grand Trunk Railway was inaugurated, a railway that would eventually link the entire country, from Halifax to Vancouver. In the same year, work commenced on the first rail link between Montreal and the south shore of the St. Lawrence River. The Victoria Bridge, 2,009 metres long, carries trains over the rushing river to this very day.

Building rail lines, manufacturing rails and engine parts, constructing railyards and maintaining the rolling stock meant recruiting labourers, engineers, and factory hands. Irish and Black labourers, in particular, arrived in Montreal in large numbers to work on the railroads. The Irish community reached 11,736 in 1851; they formed twenty percent of the city's population. The number of Black Montrealers was much smaller, but their numbers were concentrated heavily in the rail industry; many Black men worked as porters or labourers.

During the second half of the nineteenth century, the number of rail companies expanded drastically. One could travel to almost any other city or large town on the continent by rail from Montreal. In fact, new towns were built intentionally alongside railroad tracks in both Western Canada and the United States. But as the twentieth century gathered steam, a new form of overland transportation emerged to challenge the supremacy of the railroads. This was, of course, the automobile, and its counterpart, the truck. The tremendous competition for clients among the many rail companies had already destabilized the industry to a great extent before the advent of trucking; many rail companies had merged with one another. Montreal's Grand Trunk Railway had battled with the Great Western Railway, which it took over in 1884, but continued to struggle against such giants as the Canadian Pacific Railway and the Canadian Northern Railway. Finally, in 1919, suffering from an enormous burden of debt, the Grand Trunk and its subsidiary, the Grand Trunk Pacific Railway, were nationalized. In 1923, they merged with the Canadian Northern Railway to form the still-existing crown corporation the Canadian National Railway.

Montreal continues to be the headquarters of the CNR, which eventually expanded to include such subsidiaries as CN Marine, CN Telecommunications, CN Exploration, and CNX/TCN Trucking. But after World War II, much of the maintenance and manufacturing work that had been done in Montreal began to be carried out in Toronto, or further west, on the Prairies. Today, most of the railyards in central Montreal have been torn up and replaced with low-rent housing or condominiums. The Irish and Black neighbourhoods that once flourished nearby have either disintegrated or changed beyond all recognition. And while travellers still use the passenger service, Via Rail, to travel to New York, Toronto, or Halifax, the railroad no longer plays an essential role in the city's economy or in its collective psyche.

On the Prairies, trains remain crucial transportation links because grain is still transported predominantly by rail. But in Montreal, as in other major urban centres in the 1990s, service industries have taken the lead from resource-based industries, and, as a result, despite their ecological efficiency, railroads have been relegated to a second-class role in the city's economy. The slashing of Via Rail's budget by nearly fifty percent in 1989 by Canada's Conservative government was the final nail in the coffin of passenger rail service in Canada.

For those who apply Darwinian principles to the world of transportation, the superseding of ships and rail by car, truck, and airplane is simply a necessary and natural step toward improving available transportation technology. Yet there are still many sentimentalists who favour the return of trains and ships to their former positions of importance. They argue that trains forged the chain that linked the disparate regions of this huge country; cars, on the other hand, are dangerous, and tend to isolate travellers from one another. In recent years, these sentimentalists have been joined by environmentalists who argue that cars are extremely destructive to our natural surroundings. These environmentalists also offer analyses of cost effectiveness every bit as detailed and precise as those produced by the big businesses who own the shipping lines and trucking companies.

Many of these people believe that fuel-efficient high-speed trains are the key to the future of long-distance transportation.

High-speed trains are already in full use in both Europe and Japan, and a link between Montreal and Toronto that would shorten the trip from five hours to two hours has been discussed for years. But unless the various levels of government and the private sector manage to come to an agreement concerning who will provide the billions of dollars needed to construct the new system, Montreal will likely miss out on what many feel is one of the most revolutionary breakthroughs in transportation in recent years.

Hypothetical situations aside, this is unquestionably the age of the automobile, and, to an ever-greater extent, of the airplane. Montreal's highway system is well developed; many smaller highways traverse the island, while several primary axes run through the city, and are used by hundreds of thousands of people every day.

The most important highway in Canada is undoubtedly the Trans-Canada Highway, which, as its name suggests, travels over five thousand kilometres between the Atlantic and the Pacific oceans. It forks upon reaching Montreal, Autoroute 40 crossing the city's northern neighbourhoods from east to west, and Autoroute 20 travelling along the south shore of the St. Lawrence, over the Jacques Cartier Bridge into the city, and along the southern edge of the island of Montreal. While these two highways — in the city named Boulevard Metropolitain (40) and Autoroute Ville Marie (20) — carry enormous traffic loads, they were, however, poorly designed. The 40, in particular, winds and twists its way along a narrow elevated ramp with limited vision, no shoulders, and exit and entrance ramps jutting in and out of the traffic flow. Not surprisingly, accidents are frequent on certain stretches of this highway. And, of course, Montreal's snowy winters exacerbate bad driving conditions.

The major highway to the north is the Laurentian Autoroute, which is jammed on weekends with Montrealers heading to the Laurentian Mountains, where, in lush pine forests and by countless lakes, may be found thousands of cottages, and a number of attractive inns and hotels. Five main bridges link the island of Montreal with Laval on Île Jésus, and eventually with the mainland to the north: the Pie ix, the Papineau Leblanc, the Lachapelle, the Médéric Martin, and the Viau. To the south, four bridges connect Montreal and the suburban municipalities known collectively as the South Shore: the Jacques Cartier, the Champlain, the Honoré Mercier, and the Victoria. The Mercier Bridge joins the city to the Kahnawake Reserve, and was the site of an armed siege in the summer of 1990, when it was seized by Mohawks protesting the expropriation of land for a golf course on a neighbouring reserve. The struggle was a protracted one, and attracted a great deal of media attention, some of it international. At the eastern tip of Montreal, the Louis Hippolyte Lafontaine Tunnel links the island to Île Charron. The tunnel is 1.25 kilometres long, and was constructed beneath the river. And at the island's western extremity, the Île aux Tourtes Bridge crosses Lake of Two Mountains to the suburbs of Vaudreuil and Dorion.

Within the city of Montreal, the fastest and most efficient form of transportation is the Metro, the underground subway system installed for Expo 67. The Metro trains offer a smooth ride because they have rubber tires. They zoom into relatively clean and well-lit stations without the screeching and clatter that characterizes the subways of New York, London, and Toronto. The Metro currently consists of a network of 61 kilometres of underground tunnels. Its three lines extend from the northern shore of the island to Longueil on the south shore (passing under the river), and from the western community of Lasalle to close to the eastern tip of the island. The system has 65 stations.

The Metro is under the administrative authority of the Société de Transport de la Communauté Urbaine de Montréal, which also controls an extensive bus system. Montreal's public transport is a vital element in the daily lives of many Montrealers. Buses run through every neighbourhood on the island, often well into the night. Among the relatively few criticisms Montrealers have of their public transport system is the amazing frequency with which its employees vote to go on strike. In fact, the city has averaged almost a strike a year for the past 20 years. When service is suspended in the middle of one of Montreal's brutal winters, citizens may have to resort to hitchhiking and walking in the bitter cold. The regular increase in fares is another irritant for the system's users, but they

FIGURE 6

Berri-UQAM Metro Station features modern art

recognize that Montreal can't hope to escape the problem of rising costs, which also hampers public transport systems in other cities.

Finally, Montreal is served by two airports: Dorval, built in 1960 on the northwestern section of the island, and Mirabel, built in 1975 about 45 minutes north of the city. Dorval primarily handles North American flights, while flights from Mirabel generally have overseas destinations. Mirabel is an enormous ultramodern airport with a problem: it is vastly underused. It was built as one of Mayor Jean Drapeau's monumental schemes, and was supposed to be linked to the city by a high-speed train. It was to be one of North America's busiest airports. But the train was never built; the airport itself experienced astronomical cost overruns during its construction; and, most importantly, Montreal's economic strength has declined over the past 20 years. The result? A huge, inconveniently located airport that deals with fewer than 200 flights a day.

Dorval Airport, on the other hand, is small, outdated, and unpretentious. But it handles many more passengers than Mirabel, and is situated far closer to the city centre. In 1989, Dorval's air-traffic rate reached 230,000 flights, an average of about 630 per day. The airport is, however, surrounded by residential communities that protest vigorously against any suggestion that Dorval ought to be enlarged or improved upon to attract more air traffic. They complain that the planes flying overhead are disruptive enough already, and besides, Mirabel is sitting out there waiting to be used. The communities have a good argument, and have so far withstood those who want to develop Dorval Airport. But the fight is likely to last as long as the airport exists, because it is too small and too basic to be Montreal's primary airport. Mirabel, on the other hand, is simply too far away, and too expensive to maintain if only a few major airlines use it. In 1987, the administrations of the airports were consolidated so that the two are now run as a single entity, but the merger seems uneasy at best. Meanwhile, Montrealers can take comfort in the fact that they have a major airport ready to use should they require it in the future, while at present they have a convenient, fully functioning airport on the island.

4

TRADE AND COMMERCE

MONTREAL HAS ALWAYS BEEN the commercial engine of the province, and, typically, as Montreal goes, so goes Quebec. Yet in recent years this pattern has changed drastically. While the province as a whole experienced exceptional growth in the 1980s, its development rates similar to those of Japan, during the same period Montreal suffered a severe drain of capital and an unprecedented rise in unemployment.

Quebec, in recent years, has seen formidable cooperation between government and business — a cooperation that has yielded far-reaching and positive results. However, while recent government measures to stimulate the financial sector, such as the establishment of the tremendously successful Réseau d'Épargnes Action (a tax shelter designed to encourage investment in Quebec stocks), have contributed to the revitalization of the Montreal Stock Exchange, the benefits have more often accrued to companies operating outside Montreal. A provincial agenda that encourages regional development has also contributed to strengthening the provincial economy at Montreal's expense.

Another unavoidable issue is language. The speedy and thorough conversion of the language of the workplace in Quebec's commercial and financial sectors from English to French is an achievement of which many Québécois are very proud. Yet some of the measures introduced during the past several decades to foster the emergence of a francophone entrepreneurial class have also succeeded in alienating a number of Montreal's long-standing anglophone commercial institutions. In 1987, 62 per cent of francophone Quebecers were employed by a Québécois business as compared to only 47 per cent in 1961, but, at the same time, such preeminent corporations as

FIGURE 7

Sun Life Building at the corner of
Peel and René Lévesque Boulevard

Sun Life Insurance, whose monumental offices on Dominion Square were once the symbol of Montreal's business strength, have left Montreal to establish themselves in Toronto. The issue of language, and more generally of cultural difference, has been extremely important in shaping Quebec's economy. Montreal's business history is primarily a history of the accumulation of capital by its anglophone minority, and the keen resentment of that action by the francophone majority. It was this sense of grievance against the anglophone business establishment, as well as the desire to test themselves against the world, that led Montreal's francophones to heed the nationalist slogan "maître chez nous" (our own bosses), and to build a new, modern commercial infrastructure.

Beginning in the transformative years of the Quiet Revolution, Montreal's Québécois business people have risen to a position of collective prominence almost unthinkable a generation ago. In 1960, eighty percent of middle-management and sixty percent of upper-management positions were held by Montreal's anglophones, who made up only twenty percent of the city's population. By the early 1980s, fully two-thirds of upper-management positions in Quebec were held by francophones: a remarkable turnaround. Quebec now produces more business-school graduates than any other province, many coming from the University of Montreal's École des Hautes Études Commerciales. The combination of an ever-increasing pool of entrepreneurs, a responsive provincial government, and an optimistic business climate has helped to make Montreal's businesses into Canadian, and even international, powerhouses.

For example, in 1988, 160 businesses with head offices in Montreal appeared on *Fortune* magazine's list of the top 500 companies in Canada, nearly double the number of just three years earlier. And among the 50 Canadian businesses that had most rapidly increased their profitability between 1984 and 1988, 28 were Québécois, and nearly all of these were based in Montreal. Furthermore, a handful of the most powerful corporations in Canada operate out of Montreal, including BCE, Alcan, Seagram, Provigo, Hydro Quebec, Imasco, Canadian National, and Air Canada.

The provincial government has established a battery of public corporations, many of them financial institutions designed to aid Quebec's entrepreneurs. The CDP, the Caisse de Dépot et Placement du Québec (the Quebec Deposit and Investment Fund), has invested in dozens of important Montreal companies, including Bombardier, Provigo, Steinberg, and Domtar. It has also bought controlling shares in such vital Quebec businesses as Gaz Métropolitain, Noranda, and Domtar. Founded by the provincial Liberal government in 1965, the CDP is an updated version of Quebec's traditional farming credit unions. The CDP's political mandate was to use money invested in the Quebec Pension Fund to stimulate the growth of francophone companies and industries in Quebec. The CDP came into being because francophone entrepreneurs felt that the country's five major banks, all controlled by anglophone Canadians, were not interested in lending to francophone companies. In recent years, the private sector has taken up much of the burden of financing new ventures, but the CDP remains an essential source of capital for Quebec's economy.

Hydro Quebec perhaps offers the best example of how government and business have worked together in Quebec. In the early 1960s, a young René Lévesque led the Liberal government's widely publicized battle to nationalize the private electricity utilities operating in Quebec. He finally succeeded, and the result was Hydro Quebec, now Canada's second largest corporation in terms of its assets: it had over $36 billion in 1991. Hydro Quebec has over twenty thousand permanent employees, and they are responsible for keeping both Montreal and the rest of the province lit up. In 1990, Hydro Quebec's gross revenue was in excess of $5.8 billion, from over three million customer accounts. However, not all of those customers were pleased to discover later that year that their public utility was raising prices for average consumers, while at the same time secretly selling monumental amounts of electricity to 13 different multinational firms for less than half the standard price. Such scandals, along with the problems inherent in dealing with the utility's enormous bureaucracy, have kept many Québécois sceptical of Hydro Quebec's dealings, while still feeling proud of its accomplishments.

Hydro Quebec is renowned for its hydroelectric dams, notably those of the James Bay Project, which is the largest of its kind in the world. The project is situated in northern Quebec, and is intended to harness the power of a number of the rivers that flow into James and Hudson bays. The project is huge and ongoing: the rivers it involves drain about one-fifth of the province; when all its phases are complete, it could generate up to 28,000 megawatts of power; the reservoirs of the dams will eventually equal the size of Lake Ontario. The utility is currently engaged in a ferocious battle with the Cree who inhabit the region of James Bay. The Cree are insisting that they must approve plans for a new megaproject at Great Whale River before work can commence. For Hydro Quebec, anxious to invest tens of billions of dollars in the project, environmental and social concerns take a back seat to energy needs. The Cree, however, as well as many of their supporters in Canada and abroad, disagree strongly, claiming that the damage to the land and the Native way of life will be irreparable if the project is built. The fight is currently in the courts, and is likely to remain there for several years.

Hydro Quebec's policy of massive hydroelectric development, combined with the provincial government's aim of creating stronger Quebec-based commerce, led to a huge influx of money into Montreal businesses, along with many contract offers. Among the leading beneficiaries of Hydro Quebec's initiatives were Montreal's engineering firms. Whereas SNC had only $7 million in assets in 1969, the company has now become one of the most important engineering firms in the world, with hundreds of millions of dollars in contracts from both Quebec and abroad every year. Lavalin, which had been SNC's primary competitor for 20 years, built everything from subway trains to aeronautical parts. But, in 1990, Lavalin overextended itself, and was forced to sell out to archrival SNC. Despite their differing fates, however, both of these world-class engineering firms received their initial impetus from Hydro Quebec.

But not all Montreal companies have relied on provincial support for their success. Bombardier is one of Montreal's most successful engineering firms. The company was established by Joseph Armand Bombardier in 1942. His business? He invented the snowmobile, what else? From these modest beginnings, and despite the death of its founder in 1964, Bombardier has grown to become one of the world's leading builders of transportation and aerospace components. Besides manufacturing the Ski-Doo, Bombardier owns Canadair, which makes executive jets, and in 1991 bought up its more famous competitor, Lear Jets. The company also manufactures subway and other passenger trains for several countries, including Holland and Belgium. Bombardier is the forty-second largest business in Canada; its 1991 sales were close to $3 billion. The company employs over 25,000 workers in plants located just outside Montreal, and in Iceland and Austria. Even though it has had enormous worldwide success, however, many Quebecers still think of Bombardier as the company that revolutionized life in the northern wilderness with its motorized snowmobile.

Montreal is the birthplace of one of Canada's top five banks. The Bank of Montreal was founded in 1817, and is Canada's oldest chartered bank. It was originally established to bring order to the chaotic fluctuations in exchange rates between American, Portuguese, English, French, and Spanish currencies in Montreal at a time when no Canadian currency existed. All of the original nine founders of the bank were of British origin, and some years later, the Bank of Montreal would be vilified by the Patriotes (the followers of the rebellious leader of the francophone majority in the legislative assembly of Lower Canada, Louis Joseph Papineau) for its perceived threat to francophone merchants. Francophones maintained that mistrust of the Bank of Montreal — as well as of the Royal Bank, the Canadian Imperial Bank of Commerce, the Toronto Dominion Bank, and the Bank of Nova Scotia — until the development of their own banking institution, the Caisses Populaires Desjardins, in the early twentieth century.

Today, the Bank of Montreal is an enormous institution with significant loans and subsidiaries around the globe. In 1990, the Bank of Montreal made a profit of $522 million, a figure that astounded and outraged many Canadians who were fed up with paying not-so-insignificant service fees for every bank transaction. But despite the public outcry, government intervention appears unlikely. Banks are extremely powerful in Quebec, as elsewhere, and because a given bank bears the name of Montreal does not mean that it is responsive to the particular needs or demands of Montrealers.

Montreal's evolution as an important commercial centre is characterized by an independent entrepreneurial flair epitomized by the Bronfman family, Paul Desmarais's Power Corporation, and Pierre Péladeau. By far the most powerful family in Montreal is the Bronfman family, which owns a controlling interest in Seagram, one of the world's largest distilling firms. Seagram's 1990 sales alone were nearly a billion dollars, quite apart from the family's other investments. There are actually two branches of the family, each exceedingly powerful and wealthy, and each descended from the original Bronfman patriarch, Ekiel, who emigrated from Russia to Manitoba in 1889. The Seagram-owning Bronfmans are Charles, Edgar, and Phyllis, whose father Samuel built the family's fortune in the 1920s and '30s. Samuel's brother Allan's two sons, Edward and Peter, run Edper Investments, which controls financial and industrial corporations that are nearly equal in value to Seagram.

Montreal legend has it that the family's empire grew out of liquor smuggling during the era of American Prohibition. The Bronfmans vigorously deny this. In more recent times, they have contributed to Montreal's cultural life by building the Canadian Centre for Architecture (see chapter 8), and the Saidye Bronfman Centre (a cultural centre that houses a theatre, an art school, and a gallery), and by bringing the Montreal Expos baseball team to the city in 1969 (see chapter 7). After running the ball club for over 20 years without having won a championship, Sam's son Charles recently sold the team to a Montreal-based consortium for $100 million.

Another Montreal-based businessman with enormous economic influence is Paul Desmarais, a franco-Ontarian whose Power Corporation and its subsidiaries control several important Canadian financial institutions, including Investor's Group, the country's largest mutual fund. Desmarais is originally from Sudbury, where his journey from small-town entrepreneur to financial giant began. Desmarais's initial success was based on his restructuring of his father's local bus company by merging it with Provincial Transport, a much larger business. One of

Desmarais's ingenious decisions was to give his employees at Provincial Transport the exclusive distribution rights to tickets on the bus lines, and then to pay those employees in bus tickets. By so doing, he alleviated the cash crisis resulting from his takeover of the larger firm, while simultaneously gaining the loyalty of his new employees.

To this day, Desmarais remains one of the country's most successful businessmen. He recently sold his controlling interest in Montreal Trust, one of Canada's most valuable trust companies, to another Montreal-based conglomerate, BCE (Bell Canada Enterprises), for over half a billion dollars. He has also become prominent in the Montreal media industry, buying the daily newspaper *La Presse* and the top French-language radio station, CKAC. Desmarais is also represented in the insurance sector, having gained control of such major Canadian institutions as Imperial Life of Toronto and Great West Life of Winnipeg, as well as several European insurance companies.

But while Desmarais dabbles in media by controlling *La Presse*, his importance in the world of print is overshadowed by that of another Montreal financier, Pierre Péladeau. Péladeau's Québécor is now the second-largest printer in North America, having entered into a new $575 million partnership with the late Robert Maxwell's firm. Péladeau struck a typical Quebec business deal: Québécor invested 57.5 per cent of the cash for the new corporation, Maxwell's Canadian arm supplied 20 per cent, and the Caisse de Dépot et Placement du Québec kicked in the remaining 22.5 per cent. Not surprisingly, Péladeau is on the board of directors of the CDP.

Péladeau rose to his current position by buying and/or founding a string of francophone newspapers in Quebec. Starting with small suburban weeklies, he soon went on to create what would become the largest newspaper in Quebec, and the largest francophone newspaper in North America: *Le Journal de Montréal*. The paper is a brash tabloid, but it is actually among the best of Péladeau's many publications. His other great print successes include such wonders as *Allô Police* (dedicated to the most gruesome crimes of the week), *Hebdô Police* (more of the same), and a seemingly endless array of gossip magazines that dissect the lives of famous (and not-so-famous) Quebecers. There can

49

be little doubt that Pierre Péladeau is one of the most influential men in Quebec: Québécor has almost $3 billion in assets. But when his contributions to the world of publishing as well as his occasional public tirades are taken into account, the nature of his influence is questionable.

This may prompt us to wonder just what role these immensely powerful people play in Montreal's daily life. Who are they? To the vast majority of Montrealers, names such as Bronfman, Desmarais, and Péladeau are simply code words for the kind of power and wealth they can only dream of. Certainly companies such as BCE and Alcan, which employ tens of thousands of workers each, are vitally important to the evolution and even the survival of Montreal as an economic force. But despite the ties that have been created between commercial enterprises and provincial institutions in order to foster economic growth for all, decisions made at the highest levels have not generally been influenced by input from workers. Is Montreal's interest, or Quebec's, the governing interest? Obviously not, as the globalization of the world's economies leads businesses to consider moving plants from highly unionized and moderately taxed regions such as Montreal, to non-unionized and virtually unregulated third-world countries. Now that the trilateral free-trade agreement between Canada, Mexico, and the United States has become reality, there are many who fear that the shifting of plants to Mexico will be inevitable.

For while Canada, and Quebec in particular, believes that its society is essentially different from that of its American neighbours or its European ancestors, the majority of its capital remains in the hands of a few very powerful business leaders. These leaders form a power structure that is parallel to that of elected representatives, and one that is responsible only to itself. Nonetheless, Quebecers have been more successful than some in taking control of certain aspects of their lives from the powerful; labour unions, unemployment insurance, medicare, child allowance, old-age pensions, and state-subsidized universities all benefit the population as a whole. But a constant battle is waged to uphold these measures in the face of pressures that would erode them.

The Parti Québécois under René Lévesque (provincial premier from 1976–85) was determined to implement a wide variety of social-democratic reforms in Quebec, had the province achieved independence from Canada. In fact, that was the initial idea behind the nationalization of utilities and the promotion of Quebec entrepreneurs through provincial investment programs such as the CDP. Lévesque saw the government's role as one of mediator between independent capital and the average worker.

5

NEIGHBOURHOODS

IN 1945, a young and unknown author named Gabrielle Roy, a franco-Manitoban who had come to live in Montreal, published *Bonheur d'occasion* (its English translation is called *The Tin Flute*). The novel describes the life of a Québécois working-class family in the St. Henri district of Montreal. In the same year, Hugh MacLennan published *Two Solitudes*, a portrait of the cultural and economic abyss between the French and English in Montreal and the surrounding countryside. And in 1959, Mordecai Richler published *The Apprenticeship of Duddy Kravitz*, a hilarious portrait of a young Jewish entrepreneur, and of an ethnic community that had found a special niche between Montreal's two solitudes.

These three novels constitute a valuable introduction to Montreal's neighbourhoods. With only a very few exceptions, every neighbourhood in the city is reflected, to some degree, in one of the fictional neighbourhoods evoked in the novels. Despite the fact that years have elapsed since Hugh MacLennan coined the phrase, Montreal remains, for the most part, a city of two solitudes. The French still tend to live in the east, the English in the west, and the Portuguese, Italians, Greeks, Chinese, and Blacks of various ethnic origins nestle between them.

Many Montrealers would disagree with this assessment, arguing that over the past decade there have been major shifts in neighbourhood demographics, notably the migration of francophone yuppies to a number of traditionally anglophone neighbourhoods. But to an outsider, these shifts are relatively minor. The fact remains that western Montreal is predominantly anglophone, while eastern Montreal is almost exclusively francophone. Remarkably, many Montrealers live their entire lives on one side of the city without venturing more than a handful of times into the other.

To suggest, however, that nothing has changed in the past 50 years would be misleading. To an ever-greater degree, anglophone Montrealers, especially younger ones, are choosing to live farther and farther to the east. And, in contrast, even the once staunchly WASP suburbs of the West Island are now home to a significant minority of francophone professionals. The neighbourhoods are no longer as homogeneous as they once were, and most Montrealers are inwardly pleased that in their city such integration can be accomplished relatively smoothly. And this isn't surprising, really, because despite occasional periods of social unrest, Montreal has always been an exceptionally friendly and open city.

East and west are distinguished by a second, equally important factor: their degrees of wealth. Historically, western English Montreal has been far more prosperous than eastern French Montreal. Both Westmount, the city's wealthy English community, and Outremont, its French counterpart, lie to the west of St. Lawrence Boulevard, which bisects the city from north to south. Francophone entrepreneurs and professionals now tend to move to these western neighbourhoods as they attain a certain level of financial success. Yet most francophones still live in the same middle- and working-class districts in eastern and northern Montreal that they have for generations. These neighbourhoods are different from middle- and working-class neighbourhoods in other North American cities in several superficial ways, and in many more profound ones.

Middle-class neighbourhoods in North American cities are often characterized by rows of detached houses, each with a driveway and small backyard. But you won't find many of these in Montreal. Instead, most Montreal neighbourhoods have rows of brick duplexes and triplexes. Another unusual fact is that the majority of Montrealers are tenants rather than homeowners, and moving from one apartment to another is a common ritual, even for families. On 1 July, Montreal's traditional moving day, the streets are filled with cars and vans in transit from one dwelling to another, and bursting with boxes, mattresses, and all manner of household items.

FIGURE 8

Houses on Coursol Street in Saint-Henri

Let's look more closely at a few of Montreal's unique neighbourhoods. St. Henri is one of the city's oldest, and lies to the north of the old industrial district along the Lachine Canal. It differs from other lower-middle-class and working-class Québécois neighbourhoods such as Hochelaga, Ahuntsic, Cartierville, or Rosemont, only in its age, and therefore, to a certain extent, in its architecture. The latter neighbourhoods, and others like them, are actually where most Montrealers live. Yet the essential character of life in St. Henri is similar to that found in these neighbourhoods, and in such others as Pointe aux Trembles, Montreal East, and Ville d'Anjou. While St. Henri is more modern and somewhat more prosperous than Gabrielle Roy describes it in *Bonheur d'occasion*, in some respects it remains today what it was then: a small, struggling community that is nonetheless secure in its identity.

The most important landmark in St. Henri is Atwater Market, a busy outdoor and indoor market at the foot of Atwater Avenue, on the northern edge of the Lachine Canal. The large brick building, with its easily identifiable clock tower, was built in 1933 by an entrepreneur named Charles Dansereau, and immediately flourished. To this day, farmers drive to the market each day before dawn, their trucks loaded with fruit and vegetables. Their produce is eagerly snapped up by hundreds of shoppers on weekends; their numbers are more modest during the week. The market's outdoor stalls offer a visual and gastronomical feast during the fall harvest; in the winter months, vendors display maple syrup, apples, Christmas trees, and firewood. Dozens of local residents work inside the market building, some at the many butcher shops, others at the bakery, cheese, imported produce, or other speciality shops. Atwater Market has been a source of community pride since its construction.

The streets of St. Henri themselves are narrow and somewhat worn, yet they have an urban charm that transcends, or perhaps depends upon, this dilapidation. Many of the houses were built in the 1920s, when the area was prosperous, and while some have been beautifully renovated, even some that have not retain an air of sophistication and elegance that adds greatly to the district's atmosphere. St. Henri's several old-fashioned squares, with their lush trees and elaborate fountains, stand out like oases amidst the nearby factories. Some of St. Henri's streets are lined with boxlike postwar houses, but when taken as a whole, the neighbourhood's jumble of new and old is stimulating and convivial.

St. Henri has no pretensions. Its residents are workers (although these days jobs are hard to find) who probably have more in common with anglophone workers in other cities than they do with the wealthy francophones of Outremont. Yet St. Henri epitomizes several of Montreal's best qualities. These qualities are not easily seen from the outside, they must be experienced. First of all, Montreal is a relatively safe city, and even in a somewhat rough area such as St. Henri, one only rarely hears of any kind of violent confrontation. Guns and drugs simply don't play a significant role here, and, as a result, the random violence that occurs in so many American neighbourhoods is absent.

Beyond this, the residents of St. Henri, like those of other Québécois neighbourhoods, tend to live more of their lives out of doors than do their anglophone counterparts. English Canadians are generally more private and reserved than the outgoing Québécois. In St. Henri, conversations are often struck up on park benches, in corner stores, and on stoops in front of houses. Another aspect of public life in St. Henri can be found in the intricate network of back alleys that run through the area. These alleys have a life of their own, and feature one element immortalized in a popular play, *Balconville*, by Montreal playwright David Fennario. The play's title refers to the tiers of balconies that face each other behind a typical pair of triplexes, and the daily (and nightly) interaction of the tenants who use them.

St. Henri's main streets are Nôtre Dame, which is the primary commercial thoroughfare, St. Jacques, and St. Antoine. The latter two are well-travelled routes through the city, and carry too much traffic moving too fast. But that is typical of Montreal, as well: it is a city where pedestrians are trained from an early age to ignore what cars are *supposed* to do, and carefully study what they *actually* do, which is break every law in the book on a regular basis. Motorists play games of cat and mouse that seem to bother nobody, except perhaps cyclists. St. Jacques and St. Antoine streets converge at the western tip of St. Henri, and there, in a small triangular islet, stands a statue of Louis Cyr, one of Quebec's legendary heroes, and reputedly "the strongest man that ever lived." In the early years of this century, Cyr travelled the world displaying his feats of strength before kings and queens. He regularly lifted over five hundred pounds with a single finger.

St. Henri, like every other neighbourhood in the city, and in the province of Quebec for that matter, is dotted with churches. Over one hundred years ago, Mark Twain said of Montreal, "I don't like this city. You can't throw a stone without breaking a church window." Twain's remark is as accurate as it is acid; and St. Henri has several great churches to prove it.

There are, of course, more affluent French-speaking neighbourhoods in the city, Outremont being a prime example. Outremont has a European flavour, being dotted with cafés, *restos*, and chic boutiques. Laurier Street is one ventricle of the neighbourhood's commercial heart. Its *pâtisseries*, bookstores, clothing stores, and other trendy establishments primarily serve Montreal's francophone bourgeoisie and upper class. Many of Outremont's streets are lined with massive trees that shield its elegant, well-tended stone houses. Other streets contain Montreal's characteristic multiunit dwellings, but even these are among the most luxurious of their kind. Outremont only became a genuine neighbourhood at the turn of the century, when a tramway was built linking it to the city centre. Its population figures soared as wealthier Montrealers built homes in the pleasant community. Outremont has several well-tended parks, and residents also enjoy easy access to the extensive grounds of the nearby University of Montreal.

One of Montreal's most interesting qualities is the way in which its diverse communities coexist in close proximity to, or even among, one another. Outremont, for example, is home to one of the largest Hasidic Jewish communities in North America. The small synagogues or *shuls* of the Hasidim may often be found adjacent to the commercial enterprises of their drastically different neighbours. And Outremont is just a short walk from several other distinct neighbourhoods, such as Mile

FIGURE 9

*Summer sidewalk sale on Saint-Laurent
between Prince Arthur and Pine Avenue*

End, which is populated largely by members of Montreal's huge Greek community.

And Montreal's predominantly anglophone neighbourhoods — what are they like? Here again, the distinguishing factor is not so much language or culture as it is economics. Several of these neighbourhoods, such as Nôtre-Dame-de-Grâce (N.D.G.), Westmount, and Montreal West, really have more in common with Outremont than they do with working-class anglophone neighbourhoods, which are, in turn, similar in structure and lifestyle to their poorer francophone counterparts.

Westmount is a medium-sized municipality lying just west of the downtown core. It is the home of many of Montreal's anglophones, especially the wealthier ones, and has long been considered the exclusive territory of Montreal's anglo elite. Not surprisingly, its highest winding streets are lined with the most opulent and ostentatious homes. From the perspective of a francophone from Montreal North, Westmount is simply an intimidating and unpleasant reminder of how unfairly the pie has traditionally been sliced in Montreal. But within the neighbourhood itself, one can of course find a wide variety of people and ideas, and even, to a certain extent, incomes. Ultimately, Westmount's streets, shops, offices, schools, and library are as integral to central Montreal as are those of Outremont. They are simply two sides of the same coin.

The line that divides east from west in Montreal is St. Lawrence Boulevard. Ethnic communities have flourished along "the Main," as it is known, for decades, and it is no coincidence that this thoroughfare and its adjacent neighbourhoods are among the most lively and interesting in Montreal. St. Lawrence Boulevard begins in Old Montreal, among old stone warehouses and restaurants, and as it moves northward, the first neighbourhood it traverses is Montreal's small Chinatown, lined with grocery stores, gift shops, and dozens of fragrant restaurants.

At present, Chinatown consists of only a few fairly rundown residential blocks and two major intersecting commercial strips: St. Lawrence Boulevard and La Gauchetière Street. At one time, however, before the intercession of Montreal's former mayor Jean Drapeau, Chinatown was a much larger and more prosperous community. But Drapeau and his social planners considered Chinatown an eyesore because it was insufficiently "modern." As a result, during the 1960s, '70s, and '80s, the city administration placed very severe zoning restrictions on the neighbourhood, restrictions that eventually reduced its size significantly. Today, multiculturalism is more likely to be embraced as a sign of a city's vitality, and some valuable work has gone into rebuilding Chinatown. Yet it will never regain its importance to the now-scattered Chinese community.

Travelling north, the Main cuts through the city's red-light district, but soon, leaving strip bars and peep shows behind, it crosses Sherbrooke Street and enters a different world. Here the boulevard is home to chic cafés, clothing stores, nightclubs, and throngs of people — morning, noon, or night. But this section of the Main has only recently become a trendy area for patrons of the posh. Look a little harder, and perhaps a block or two further north, jammed between these new arrivals you can still find plenty of old-timers. You'll find them in their Hungarian sausage shops, Jewish jewellery stores, Polish parcel-service booths and vitamin dispensaries, fish markets, tombstone-grinding yards, poolrooms, delicatessens, and bakeries. What makes the Main so enjoyable, even to someone who has lived there for years, is that the more you look, the more you find.

The Main is also home to dozens of art galleries, many of which can be found in three restored prewar office buildings: the Balfour, Cooper, and Berman buildings. These edifices house not only galleries, but the offices of many of the city's cultural movers and shakers. So if you're looking for work as an actor, dancer, musician, comedian, or anything else in the entertainment world, chances are you'll find yourself in one of those buildings, or perhaps in one of the many nearby cafés frequented by students and artists. Montreal is one of the few North American cities left with a genuine Bohemian community, and its home is the Main.

Moving farther north still, the boulevard passes two small parks, a block apart. The first one, Place des Amériques, resembles a Latin-American plaza, and was built to reflect the recent arrival of many Salvadorans, Nicaraguans, and other Latin Americans in the community. A block away is a Portuguese version of the same sort of community square, Parc du Portugal. These parks are the current city administration's attempt to rectify the mistakes of the past with respect to ethnic Montrealers, and they have been well-received by the communities for whom they were intended. Gestures such as the creation of these small parks are important to members of ethnic communities, who may otherwise feel left out of Montreal's dominant anglo-franco dialogue.

The Main continues northward, undergoing a constant series of transformations as it passes through one neighbourhood after another. In Little Italy — home of Atwater Market's more European-flavoured north-end counterpart, the bustling Jean Talon Market — the boulevard is lined with restaurants, gelaterias, and coffee bars, where members of the Italian community gather to debate current affairs and soccer scores. The excitement on this stretch of the Main is palpable during the World Cup soccer competition. The boulevard finally comes to a halt on the north shore of the island, effectively linking the port of Montreal with the Rivière des Prairies, and forming a highly permeable border between Montreal's east and west sectors.

Montreal's downtown, to the west of the southern section of St. Lawrence Boulevard, has remained intact. Relatively few blocks have been torn down to make way for skyscrapers, and the city's centre continues to function as a commercially successful neighbourhood while at the same time housing a residential community. Montreal has not, therefore, succumbed to the all-too-common pattern of abandoning the inner city for suburbia; downtown commerce is still vital — it has not taken flight to suburban shopping malls. Montrealers still go downtown. A lot. Significant numbers still live in their city, not outside it, or on its edges, or in highrises above it. They don't fear their downtown, they embrace it, and, as a result, Montreal's social fabric has continued to withstand the wear and tear that has torn so many other cities apart.

6

EDUCATION

IN A SENSE, Montreal's schools are no different than its buildings, its neighbourhoods, or its industries. As each generation develops and implements reforms — some minor, some more ambitious — the city's schools are slowly transformed. But beneath even the most radical reforms one can discern traces of earlier aims and methods. And so it is that today Montreal's complex school system reflects in almost equal measure the influences of British administrators, the French Roman Catholic clergy, and the nationalist reformers of both the provincial Liberal Party and the Parti Québécois.

Remarkably, the reforms that brought Quebec's educational policies in line with those of the rest of the developed world occurred only in the early 1960s, as part of the fundamental reassessment of Quebec society known as the Quiet Revolution. Between 1960, when the Liberal Party, under the leadership of Jean Lesage, won a majority of seats in the provincial legislature, and 1966, when the party was narrowly defeated by the revived Union Nationale, a massive redefinition of governmental policies and practices was achieved, affecting virtually every aspect of Quebec society. One of the most important areas subject to this reform was education, and there can be no doubt that changes were sorely needed.

Prior to the 1960s, education in Quebec was controlled almost exclusively by religious institutions. The seminaries of the Sulpician, Jesuit, and other orders had been the sole francophone educational institutes in Quebec for over two hundred years, and in 1960, the entire francophone educational system was still governed by the Catholic Council of Bishops. The anglophone schools, meanwhile, were under the administrative supervision of the Protestant church. Despite their denominational character, the Protestant schools were far less oriented towards religious instruction than their Catholic counterparts, and a much more significant number of their students went on to postsecondary instruction (often at Montreal's McGill University or Sir George Williams University) than did those enrolled in the Catholic system. In contrast, higher education, unless it was specifically religious in nature, was discouraged by Catholic teachers, many of whom feared that exposure to worldly studies would weaken their students' religious faith. As a result, instruction in the sciences and technologies was virtually nonexistent in many francophone schools; these institutions emphasized religious studies to a degree unmatched anywhere else in Canada.

Yet it had been the British, in the early eighteenth century, who first introduced a form of popular education to Quebec, seeing it as a tool to indoctrinate and assimilate the francophone majority in the recently conquered colony. Although British-organized schools catered only to a minority of the boys in the province, their intrusion was actively resisted by the Catholic church, and by the francophone populace, who refused to be assimilated. For the most part, British influence was felt in the anglophone communities, for whom McGill University was established in 1821.

So when the Liberals took power in 1960, their aim was clear: revolutionize educational policies in order to offer the same opportunities to students in Montreal, and in Quebec as a whole, as those afforded to students elsewhere. Their reforms were widely resisted by powerful members of the church, who defeated repeated attempts to secularize and amalgamate the denominational school boards. Even today, the Commission des Écoles Catholiques de Montréal and the Protestant School Board of Greater Montreal retain control of the city's schools. Many progressive policies were finally adopted, however, and in terms of the quality of the education they offer, Montreal's schools are now comparable to those in any other major city. Furthermore, education is now a provincial responsibility, so whatever standards and systems are applied in Montreal are also applied throughout Quebec, and vice versa.

But while religious conflicts have, for the most part, been

resolved since the Quiet Revolution, in recent years a new bone of contention has caused an enormous political and emotional rift in educational policy: the issue of language rights. After the Parti Québécois rose to power with an unexpected landslide victory in the 1976 provincial election, Quebec nationalists took education in hand and sought to use it as a tool to reaffirm the primacy of the French language in Quebec. Their quite reasonable fear was that, as North Americans, surrounded by a 270-million-strong sea of anglophones, young Quebecers would inevitably discard their linguistic heritage and adopt English unless drastic defensive measures were taken. And, their argument continued, once a language goes — as did Basque and Catalan in Spain, Breton in France, and Gaelic in Ireland — the culture soon follows. All that remains is another half-remembered heritage and a nearly forgotten tongue, spoken only by the elderly and lovers of esoterica.

The solution of the Parti Québécois to this perceived menace was to legislate the teaching of language. Bill 101, enacted in 1977, decreed that only children whose parents had attended school in Quebec, in English, would henceforth be allowed to attend English schools. Anybody else — all francophones, all immigrants, all Canadians moving to Quebec from other provinces — would be required by law to send their children to French schools, where they would receive only minimal exposure to English. Needless to say, such measures sparked a storm of controversy, and remain controversial to this day. For years, parents "smuggled" their children into English schools, until eventually the guidelines were revised to permit certain students to go to school in English. (In 1987, the Bourassa government passed Bill 58, which granted amnesty to those "smuggled" children.) But the law remains essentially intact, and the resentment felt by many towards it persists.

One of the arguments used to criticize the law was that immigrants arriving in Quebec and forced to learn French would be prevented from functioning in a continental context. And, it was pointed out, they would likely find some means of learning English at the same time. Yet, in this respect at least, Bill 101 has been successful. Vietnamese, Chilean, and Polish children, along with those from countless other countries, have all gone to school in French for many years now, and the result is that across Montreal there are large numbers of young men and women who speak both French and English fluently, and who feel much more at home in Montreal than they might have had they learned French as one of several subjects in an English school. English schools, however, have now responded to increased demands for better French instruction by creating an array of French immersion programs for their students, and these students are now able to function in French with much greater ease than their parents did as school children. Many immigrant children in Montreal attend École St. Luc, which is renowned for its immersion programs geared towards refugees and immigrants. This school can lay claim to having 84 different maternal languages spoken by its students, a record probably unmatched by many large universities. St. Luc truly reflects the cultural mosaic of the city, and its students all use French as their common language. What was initially a controversial experiment has become a unique and successful program.

Another aspect of Quebec education that distinguishes it from that of other places is its grouping of grades. In Montreal schools, and in those of the rest of the province, elementary school consists of grades 1 through 6, and high school consists of grades 7 through 11. At this point, a student may voluntarily leave school, or continue on to one of 10 CEGEPs on the island. These CEGEPs (collèges d'enseignement générale et professionel) are designed to offer students flexibility in either their preuniversity or vocational studies. Preuniversity programs are usually two years in duration, while vocational programs, such as mechanical engineering, forest management, or jewellery design, are usually three.

CEGEPs have many advantages over traditional high schools. They provide students aged 16 to 17 with the responsibility of selecting their own school, educational direction, and specific courses (students choose from a broad range of disciplines including social sciences, pure and applied sciences, literature and languages, and art and music). As a result, students are able to meet people from different neighbourhoods and backgrounds, which can be as essential a learning experience as going to classes. Attending CEGEP also makes students feel far more mature than they did in high school, or than they might have felt in a different system. The CEGEP system recognizes that by the age of 16, students need space to grow — that they are too old to be grouped with 14-year-olds, but too young to compete with 18- and 19-year-old students about to enter university. In essence, CEGEP proves to students that society recognizes that they are no longer children, they are young adults, and treats them accordingly. The CEGEP system is perhaps the most successful educational innovation Quebec has put forward.

Montreal has three English and seven French public CEGEPs. These are open to any student, and cost very little to attend. Several private CEGEPs exist, but even these, for the most part, are relatively inexpensive. The largest public CEGEPs are Dawson College, on the English side, which has a student body that ranges from five thousand to eight thousand, and de Maisonneuve, Vieux Montréal, and Ahuntsic, on the French side, all of which have approximately five thousand students each.

The traditional North American infatuation with school sports and school spirit is utterly lacking in Montreal, where even varsity hockey teams play to empty arenas, if they play at all. Many CEGEPs do not even have competitive-sports teams; they have active political and cultural organizations on campus instead. Many militant nationalist groups have traditionally found widespread support among CEGEP students, who, in the mid-1970s, mounted massive demonstrations. Of course, in more recent times, political will of that magnitude has largely disappeared from Montreal's college campuses, as it has from campuses across North America.

Montreal has four universities — two English and two French. They are McGill University, Concordia University, the University of Montreal, and the University of Quebec at Montreal (UQAM). McGill is the oldest, having gained its university status in 1821. It had operated since 1801 as the Royal Institute for the Advancement of Learning, and was permitted to expand by a posthumous endowment of $10,000 from James McGill. McGill also donated his extensive estate, located at what was then the northern extremity of the city, but which has since become the heart of the downtown area.

Today, McGill's enrolment is close to 25,000. It owns a large

FIGURE 10

*McGill University's lower campus
as seen from Sherbrooke Street*

network of buildings, many of them flanking the southern slope of Mount Royal. But while McGill is undoubtedly one of the most physically interesting and attractive universities in Canada, its reputation as an important learning institution is its true strength. Over the years, such eminent figures as neurologist Wilder Penfield, humorist Stephen Leacock, and physicist Ernest Rutherford have taught there. McGill is perhaps most renowned for its faculty of medicine, which has attracted researchers from around the world. Other faculties with strong records include music, architecture, physics, meteorology, philosophy, and law, to name just a few.

In 1974, Concordia University was formed by the amalgamation of two long-established institutions: Sir George Williams University (founded in 1848) and Loyola College (founded in 1899). Concordia's enrolment is approximately equal to McGill's, although a larger percentage of its students attend on a part-time basis, many in the evening. While McGill's reputation has long overshadowed that of poorer, physically modest Concordia, the latter has grown steadily in size, increased its resources, and produced a steady number of graduates since its creation. The university is housed on two campuses, one consisting of a scattered group of downtown office buildings and townhouses, and the other of the stately Loyola College buildings, on spacious grounds in Montreal West.

Concordia has received widespread recognition for a number of its faculties, including fine arts, commerce, political science, and English. A number of highly successful colleges and institutes were also established within it in the late 1970s, among them the Liberal Arts College, the Simone de Beauvoir Institute for Women's Studies, and the Lonergan Institute for Religious Studies. These colleges regularly attract high-quality students and professors, and are one of Concordia's more inspired contributions to the city's spectrum of educational possibilities.

Montreal's two French universities can be roughly compared to their English counterparts in that the University of Montreal (founded in 1876), like McGill, has long been an important and refined institution, whereas the University of Quebec at Montreal (founded in 1968), like Concordia, is the new kid on the block.

FIGURE 11

*University of Montreal: aerial
view of the main pavilion*

U of M is Quebec's largest university, with a total enrolment of approximately fifty thousand. It is the most prestigious francophone university in Quebec, and numbers generations of Montreal's francophone business and political leaders among its graduates. U of M's most important institutes include the École des Hautes Études Commerciales and the École Polytechnique. The latter, a highly respected engineering school, gained general renown under tragic circumstances when 14 of its women students were murdered there by a deranged antifeminist gunman in 1989. U of M has faculties of law, medicine, literature, and dozens of others in the pure, applied, and social sciences.

The University of Quebec at Montreal is a far more recently established, and far more flexible institution than U of M. Founded in 1968, UQAM fosters research in virtually every possible academic discipline. Many of these, such as sexology, wouldn't be accepted at traditional schools such as U of M. Nonetheless, UQAM is a serious institution, with scientific and business research institutes, extensive arts programs, and a wide array of academic disciplines. The school itself is made up of a half-dozen campuses located across the province. The largest of these is in Montreal, and it is situated in a monumental yet nonforbidding building complex on St. Denis Street. A degree from UQAM is not yet equal in status to one from U of M, yet many students prefer the more adventurous and less intimidating climate of the newer school.

Taken as a whole, Montreal's CEGEPs and universities provide a remarkable range of educational opportunities, and all at a minimal cost to students. As is the case throughout Canada, the bulk of educational costs is covered by taxpayers, and while tuition fees have been slowly rising in recent years, they have not become prohibitive for most students. A system of loans and bursaries for students in financial need helps to give access to postsecondary education to as many young people as possible.

7

CULTURE AND LIFESTYLE

IN NO OTHER DOMAIN is Montreal's uniqueness, its extraordinary vitality and freshness, as apparent as in its cultural life. For it is Montreal's artists, dancers, painters, playwrights, musicians, authors, and cultural entrepreneurs who most readily unite its disparate ethnic and linguistic communities. Just as New Orleans is deservedly famous for its mingling of races and cultures in the early twentieth century, a mingling that produced, among other things, jazz music, so have Montreal's two primary cultures, enlivened by recent immigrants from around the globe, created a cultural milieu unparalleled in kind, if not in size, by any other in North America.

What sets Montreal apart from any other major city is its French-Canadian cultural heritage. This heritage, in both its urban and rural manifestations, is a hybrid of Euro-Latin and North American influences. In Montreal, it manifests itself as a desire for intimacy and openness, a striving for the new, the revolutionary; such qualities are not generally considered to inform the more conservative tradition of the English community. Montreal is home, for example, to an active and remarkably successful artistic avant-garde. Exciting work is being done in the fields of music (the work of René Lussier and Serge Garant, for example), film (Denys Arcand, Léa Pool, Gilles Carle), dance (Tangente, Marie Chouinard), and theatre (Carbonne 14), all of which are largely dominated by French Canadians. The anglophone community, however, provides Montrealers with a link to the mainstream culture of North America and its myriad of ideas, styles, and techniques.

To some degree, the French and English artistic communities are distinct from one another, and it may at times seem strange that there is so little overlap. Yet for bilingual Montrealers anxious to explore an alternative cultural milieu, the city offers constant stimulation. More and more, French and English artists and audiences are discovering that their interests are complementary, and the results are auspicious for the entire city. Add to this the fact that in the past decade theatre groups and concert series featuring representatives of Montreal's allophone communities have sprung up with an impressive frequency, and the picture grows even more alluring. If Montrealers can one day attain a truly cooperative spirit within their divergent artistic communities, their city might well become one of the most exciting in the world in the area of the arts. At present, however, this promise remains obscured by a history of cultural exclusivity, and by too many still-active cultural prejudices.

There can be little doubt that Montreal is at its best when its people congregate to enjoy each other's company in a creative environment. In fact, the real key to understanding Montreal is the recognition that Montrealers simply love to congregate, period. They will leap at any chance to come out in large numbers for a celebration, or *fête*. There are *fêtes* of one kind or another all summer long, and quite a few in winter too. Because the city is relatively such a safe and friendly one, and because individual rights, appearances, and attitudes are so casually accepted, huge crowds will often gather.

Take, for example, one of the city's most enjoyable events: the spring and summer Benson and Hedges International Fireworks Festival. This event, which is held for eight consecutive Wednesdays and Saturdays every May and June, is staged on St. Helen's Island (just opposite the port of Montreal). Because the fireworks are both powerful and beautiful, and because they are perfectly visible from the shore of the St. Lawrence River, Montrealers consistently show up in enormous numbers to watch the displays from across the water, and thus avoid the admission fee charged at the site. In fact, the city administration has obligingly closed the giant Jacques Cartier Bridge to traffic an hour or two before the event so that upwards of 100,000 people can walk onto it and see the fireworks from an ideal vantage point. The festival has been going on for years now, and in good weather can still attract throngs of teenagers, families with infants in strollers, and even motorcycle gangs — people whose only common interest is the spectacular show. Despite the enormous crowds and minimal policing, accidents are rare and fights or robberies are almost unheard of.

Another example of a popular Montreal crowd scene is the annual International Jazz Festival. During the entire 12-day festival, parts of several major downtown streets are closed to traffic. Stages are set up outside, as are bleachers and beer and souvenir stands. At noon each day the party begins. There are over three hundred free outdoor concerts. Approximately one million people come out to enjoy the music and the atmosphere over the course of the festival. The International Jazz Festival has become one of Montreal's most important tourist attractions by consistently offering good times and excellent music for days on end, much of it at no cost. Of course, there are many indoor concerts given by internationally renowned performers, and the steep ticket prices for these events help offset the costs of the festival.

The Just for Laughs Festival, which follows the jazzfest and lasts even longer, commandeers three long blocks of St. Denis Street in mid-July. The streets fill with acrobats, street comedians, mimes, jugglers, clowns, magicians, and every other species of street entertainer on the planet, all in town to perform at the world's largest comedy festival. For the unfortunate people who live on St. Denis, the crowds still milling about at three or four o'clock in the morning can be tiresome, but that is the price they pay for living in the nightlife centre of the province.

And so it goes: it seems as though each time a new festival is hatched Montrealers are happy to attend — in droves. There is the Montreal World Film Festival, which draws close to 300,000 film buffs annually, and there are several smaller film festivals such as the Festival de Film et Vidéo Contemporain, the Vues d'Afrique, and the Festival of Films on Art. There is the Festival International de Nouvelle Danse, the Festival du Théâtre des Amériques, and the Carifête, a festival and spectacular parade organized by Montrealers of Caribbean origin to celebrate the culture they embrace.

Many locals believe it is the harshness of the city's winters

FIGURE 12

Crowds at Montreal's International Jazz Festival

that sends Montrealers out to play with a vengeance as soon as the snow melts. Whatever the reason, festivals are consistently popular in Montreal. While in some cities such events might simply be staged tourist attractions, in Montreal this plainly isn't the case.

Montreal's culture is not, of course, limited to outdoor festivals. The city is home to vibrant artistic communities of every kind, each of which is an integral part of the city's cultural landscape. Montreal offers a wide range of musical venues, from small Old Montreal *boîtes de nuit* to major halls and clubs such as the Spectrum and Théâtre St. Denis. Montrealers flock to these establishments to hear their favourite local and international stars. A substantial number of the province's most popular musicians make Montreal their home. Among the most famous groups in Québécois musical history is Montreal's Harmonium, which performed its mellifluous compositions across Europe and North America in the late 1970s. The group disbanded in the early 1980s, but Serge Fiori and Richard Séguin, the group's songwriters, have maintained successful musical careers. Other giants of Québécois music include Gilles Vigneault, the leader of a generation of *chansonniers* whose songs captured the hearts and imaginations of Quebecers. His "Mon Pays" remains an anthem for all French Canadians: *"Mon pays ce n'est pas un pays, c'est l'hiver"* ("my land is not a land, it is winter"). In recent years, Richard Desjardins has been hailed as Vigneault's heir, and his concerts are packed whenever he appears in Montreal. Michel Rivard, Daniel Lemieux, Marjo, Robert Charlebois, and many other singer-songwriters have achieved legendary status in Quebec, and, to an ever-greater extent, in France. It is unfortunate that they remain virtually unknown outside the francophone world, because their songs are often passionate and musically compelling.

The Montreal Symphony Orchestra is among the best in the world; it has performed in the world's most prestigious concert halls, from Tokyo to Texas. The symphony's home is Salle Wilfrid Pelletier in the city's Place des Arts complex. This impressive arts centre — its design was loosely based on that of Lincoln Centre in New York City — is the site of a multitude of concerts, ballets, operas, plays, and other shows every year.

Montreal also boasts a number of other first-class musical institutions, among them the Montreal Metropolitan Orchestra, the McGill Chamber Orchestra, the Opera of Montreal, and les Grand Ballets Canadiens.

One could write an entire book about Montreal's multicultural music scene. Before leaving the subject, however, it is important to note that Montreal's Black community has an exceptionally vital musical heritage, and was home for 40 years to one of the most exciting jazz scenes in North America. Oscar Peterson was only one of many local musicians whose skills were lavishly praised by the likes of Billie Holiday, Duke Ellington, and Count Basie, all of whom performed in Montreal regularly throughout the 1930s and 40s. It was a planning decision made by the Drapeau city administration that destroyed the spirited neighbourhood that was home to the city's jazz scene. In 1967, the city constructed the Ville Marie Expressway, and it ran right through Little Burgundy. The small community never recovered.

In 1989, construction began on a new home for the Montreal Museum of Contemporary Art, which had previously been located in an area of the city that has very poor public access. The new building is downtown, adjacent to Place des Arts. Although critics complain that it is too monolithic to fit gracefully into its surroundings, promoters of the new site insist that the move was necessary. The Montreal Museum of Contemporary Art has an impressive record as an advocate of the latest developments in painting, photography, sculpture, and mixed-media installations. Despite some observations that the building might have been better designed, its relocation to the heart of the city will elevate its profile: the new museum has more exhibition space, and now has room to display its permanent collection and host larger travelling shows; and the public can now get to the museum without difficulty.

Another of the city's major cultural institutions, alongside the Canadian Centre for Architecture (see chapter 8) and the Montreal Museum of Contemporary Art, is the Montreal Museum of Fine Arts. Founded in 1947, the museum has recently undergone a major expansion. The museum is housed in an impressive neoclassical stone building on Sherbrooke

Street; recently, a far more modern wing was opened directly across the street. The MMFA has a small and diverse collection of works by such painters as Holbein, Rembrandt, Dali, and Modigliani, as well as others by important Canadian and Québécois painters such as Jack Bush and Jean-Paul Riopelle. Several exhibits of international importance have been hosted by the museum, including that of Jacqueline Picasso's private collection of her late husband's works. These works had never been publicly shown, and the exhibit opened at the MMFA.

Montreal is also home to a number of smaller museums with collections and installations that reflect a broad range of interests. Among them are: the Museum of Decorative Arts in Château Dufresne, next to the Olympic Stadium in the city's east end; the Montreal Museum of Archaeology and History at Pointe à Callière in Old Montreal; and the McCord Museum of Canadian History on Sherbrooke Street opposite McGill University. The McCord Museum recently underwent a three-year renovation, and has emerged rejuvenated; its exhibition space has more than doubled. Of special interest is the museum's Notman Photographic Archives, and there is now ample room to display specimens from it. Commercial photographer William Notman opened a studio in Montreal in 1856, and immediately met with great success. Studio staff members travelled the country, capturing images of the construction of the Canadian Pacific Railway, and of the life of the Native peoples of the West, among other things. At home in Montreal, the studio became famous for its portraits and for its composite pictures, made by cutting and pasting together up to about three hundred individual photographs. The Notman Archives offer us a glimpse into an earlier, fascinating stage in the life of Montreal and Canada itself.

The city's large exposition halls — the Montreal Convention Centre, Place Bonaventure, and the Palais de la Civilisation — attract hordes of visitors each year by mounting a wide range of shows. For example, Place Bonaventure is the home of a huge annual Christmas exhibit and sale of handicrafts made by Quebec artisans, and the Palais de la Civilisation recently hosted a show entitled "Rome: 1,000 Years of Civilization," featuring hundreds of archaeological treasures, many of which were being publicly exhibited for the first time. It was the largest exhibition of its kind ever held in North America.

There are at least 10 major theatre companies in Montreal; offerings are particularly bountiful for French-speaking theatre lovers. The Théâtre du Nouveau Monde and the Théâtre du Rideau Vert (which recently acquired a new, 426-seat hall) both specialize in classical repertory and contemporary theatre pieces. The 36-year-old Théâtre de Quat'Sous, housed in an old synagogue off the Main, is a showcase for the works of young Québécois playwrights. The Théâtre St. Denis, while doubling as a concert hall, frequently serves as a venue for touring Broadway productions. The Centaur Theatre, in the former stock-exchange building in Old Montreal, is really two theatres under a single roof. The Centaur is the city's best-known English-language theatre. The Saidye Bronfman Centre theatre also presents a series of English plays each year, as well as two plays in Yiddish. A variety of productions by a host of smaller theatrical companies round out the city's vibrant theatre scene at any given time of the year.

Another kind of theatrical company has its home base in Montreal, although it has logged countless kilometres on its extremely successful tours of North America, Europe, and Japan since it was established in 1982. The Cirque de Soleil, of which Montrealers are justifiably very proud, is so unique and appealing that it has spawned a host of imitators in recent years. Circus founder Guy Laliberté made three intriguing artistic choices that, in retrospect, seem inspired: the troupe performs under an old-fashioned big top, not in arenas (with its bright blue and yellow stripes the huge tent is a summer landmark at the Old Port when the circus is in town); no animals are used (no lions or lion tamers, no dancing bears or elephants); and, finally, many techniques of contemporary theatre are incorporated into the spectacle. The Cirque du Soleil, ever in need of talented new performers, uses Montreal's National Circus School as its training ground. The school attracts children and adolescents from around the world who come to learn trapeze, juggling, tightrope walking, tumbling, clowning, contortion, and a host of other skills. The school is one of the most successful cultural initiatives in recent Montreal history.

FIGURE 13

The Cirque du Soleil in action: the Baroques

FIGURE 14

Maison de la Culture du Plateau Mont-Royal

Museums, symphonies, and theatre companies are of great value to any city, indeed they are considered essential by many. But great cultural institutions play a very small role in the lives of the vast majority of people. In order to meet the needs of those living in communities away from the city centre, or those who cannot afford to pay admission prices to most cultural events and institutions, the city established *Les Maisons de la Culture*. These *maisons*, of which there are currently 12 (more are on the way), have proven fabulously popular.

They are situated in buildings that are already integrated into a community — old police stations, firehalls, or offices. Each is renovated to house a library (complete with video and audio equipment), an art gallery, and a small auditorium. Some have workshop areas. Local artists and musicians are hired to exhibit and perform throughout the network of *maisons*, and their concerts and exhibitions are always free. What began as an experiment has become one of the mainstays of Montreal's cultural life: hundreds of concerts and events are held annually at each *maison*. It is important to note that most of the *maisons* are located in working-class areas, because the residents of these areas would otherwise have little opportunity to hear and see the work that is now brought to their doorsteps. The *maisons* have also been a tremendous boon to Montreal's performers, who can now perform a 15-concert tour of their own city and be paid by the city administration. The artists and performers chosen to work in the *maisons* range from opera singers and harpsichordists to the most extreme avant-gardists; this emphasizes the city's democratic commitment to bringing art — all art — to anyone who wants it.

Montrealers have always had a healthy appetite for good times, good food, and good drink, and they are willing to stay up late to indulge it. As a result, Montreal's bars are open until 3 o'clock in the morning, later than anywhere else in Canada. Many nightclubs cater to a young crowd, and it is common to find even 15- or 16-year-olds in some downtown spots on weekends. Montrealers don't consider this immoral. They simply see it as an expression of more liberal social values than those held elsewhere in Canada, or the United States for that matter. Only rarely do these teenagers get into serious trouble.

In fact, many Montrealers would argue that in places where the legal drinking age is 19, and where teenagers are not permitted to participate in adult social life, young people are apt to choose far more dangerous methods of satisfying their adventurous urges than getting dressed up and going dancing. In Montreal, generally speaking, adolescents grow up quickly, but many grow up with a relatively high degree of sophistication. And while at times parents may worry, most seem content to allow their children this freedom — as long as the city remains safe.

Sports are a popular pastime in Montreal, as they are elsewhere, yet Montrealers' particular love of winter sports is matched only by that of the Scandinavians. During the long, cold winters, skis, skates, snowshoes, toboggans, and hockey sticks become as important to many residents as a pair of warm boots. Girls and boys often spend hours a day playing shinny (pickup hockey), or skating at the local rink. On weekends, Beaver Lake, the frozen pond atop Mount Royal, attracts thousands of skaters, from children who whip along like tiny Wayne Gretzkys, to new Canadians, strapped into skates for the first time, who balance tentatively at the edge of the ice. The beautifully designed Lafontaine Park, several kilometres east of Mount Royal, has another popular skating lake.

Mount Royal also has several well-used tobogganing slopes, from which the whoops and hollers of children can be heard for what seems like miles. Cross-country skiers love the mountain too, for it has 18 kilometres of groomed trails accessible 24 hours a day. It's thrilling to set out for the mountain at midnight, strap on a pair of skis, and glide through the woods above the heart of the city by moonlight.

Softball, soccer, and cycling are the most popular athletic activities in the summer. The only thing to rival them is simply walking around, which Montrealers do nearly 365 days a year in large numbers. Montreal has an impressive network of bicycle paths with a total length of 304 kilometres. The city's cycling lobby is still not satisfied, however, and has been advocating a broad range of improvements and extensions. Some of the existing paths are scenic and very enjoyable to ride. One well-tended path follows the Lachine Canal from Old Montreal through the old industrial district and out to the shore of the St. Lawrence River. (Some Montrealers have proposed that the canal itself be turned into a skating rink, like the 14 kilometre Rideau Canal in Ottawa, yet at this point little action has been taken to turn an intriguing plan into reality.) The riverfront area is ideal for cycling, and, during the winter, also serves as a cross-country ski run.

Spectator sports are, in Montreal (as they are virtually everywhere), a major preoccupation, but the energy of many Montreal sports fans is reserved exclusively for hockey and, to a lesser extent, baseball. It is often said that hockey in Montreal isn't a sport, it's a religion. If so, then the local hockey gods are unquestionably the Montreal Canadiens, the winningest team in professional hockey history. The Canadiens are one of the National Hockey League's four original franchises, but predate the league by eight years, having been founded way back in 1909. Since then, the Canadiens have won the Stanley Cup as league champions 21 times, and have come to symbolize hockey excellence the world over.

The Montreal team's dominance in hockey is akin to that of the Boston Celtics in basketball or the New York Yankees in baseball. But can even those great franchises match the Canadiens' awesome achievements? The team has won the Stanley Cup 14 times in 24 years (between 1955 and 1979); they had an 80-game season in which they lost only 8 games; and they are the only major sports franchise in the world to maintain a winning record on the road over its entire history! Montreal's stars include the likes of Howie Morenz, Georges Vézina, Maurice Richard, Jean Béliveau, Larry Robinson, Guy Lafleur, and legions of other hall-of-famers. The team's home since 1924 has been the Montreal Forum, a hockey shrine last renovated in 1968. Now there are plans for a new forum to be constructed a few blocks southeast of the old one at the corner of Atwater Avenue and Ste. Catherine Street.

Imagine trying to grow up in the shadow of the Montreal Canadiens. That is exactly the problem that has faced the Expos, Montreal's National League baseball team. No matter how hard they try, the boys of summer are always overshadowed by the boys of winter. And because the hockey season now lasts until June, baseball fever doesn't usually hit Montreal until mid-summer. And, typically, by that time the Expos are already irrevocably mired in last place. As a result, fan attendance has been among the lowest in the majors for several years.

During the franchise's early years, baseball was extremely popular in Montreal. This was in part because it was something of a novelty, but also because the Expos played their home games in what was essentially a minor-league ballpark. Jarry Park only held thirty thousand people, which meant that the fans were packed in so close to the action that they could literally reach out and touch the pitchers warming up in the bullpen. It was great fun, and it wasn't all that important if the team won or lost.

After the 1976 Olympics, however, the Expos made a disastrous move to the Olympic Stadium — disastrous because the Big O is as cold and intimidating as Jarry Park had been warm and intimate. The Expos had a few good years in their new stadium due to the excellent team they fielded in the early 1980s. That team featured all-stars such as Tim Raines, Gary Carter, and André Dawson. But when the club consistently failed to win the big games, losing several times on the last few days of the season, Montrealers became disheartened. After all, if the Expos weren't winning the fans could always look forward to hockey. Now, with a poor team and an unappealing stadium, the Expos' future in Montreal is cloudy. Many players have criticized the city, saying it's not really a baseball town. And, while this may well be true, should the Expos ever leave, a great many Montrealers would be greatly saddened by their departure. One heartening note is the team's turnaround performance in 1992; during that season they took second place in their division.

Montreal has four daily newspapers. Of all North American cities, only New York can equal that number. *La Presse* is the largest and most comprehensive French-language paper, and the smaller *Le Devoir* is the one Montrealers choose for more in-depth analysis of current affairs. The at-times-sensationalistic *Journal de Montréal* is the most popular. The Montreal *Gazette* is the city's only remaining English daily, and is also one of the oldest newspapers in North America; it was founded in 1785.

Montreal's cultural life is varied and vibrant. It reflects its residents' profound appreciation of the arts, in both their traditional and modern forms, and their love of the outdoors — and in particular their love of being outdoors in the company of others. Montreal is a city that loves the summertime, yet also makes the most of winter. It is a city whose people enjoy participating in community events, are not afraid to try something new, and have a deep attachment to their Québécois cultural heritage. Even anglophone Montrealers, for all their stubborn resistance to Quebec nationalism, have always known that it is the Québécois spirit that has made living in Montreal so worthwhile. Without it, the city is unimaginable. With it, and with the contributions of anglophone and immigrant cultures, Montreal is a charming and sometimes dazzling assemblage of sights, sounds, smells, tastes, and experiences.

8

LANDMARKS AND SPECIAL PLACES

GROWING UP IN A CITY — any city — one finds that the places one considers special grow and change as well. To a child, the front steps of a house, the backyard, or the school yard might be special. An adolescent exploring a city by bicycle or subway suddenly discovers distant and mysterious neighbourhoods, and downtown with all its excitement. When one reaches adulthood, the city changes again. It becomes a place in which to work, struggle, and build a life. A special place for an adult might be a favourite restaurant or museum. And yet, despite transformations that aging brings about, we never quite lose those feelings of affection for the special places of our childhood and adolescence. Our memories of these places stay with us: they inform our daily sense of the city that surrounds us, that we inhabit, and they provide an ongoing point of connection with other city natives whose experiences have overlapped with our own.

Montreal, too, had a childhood, and an adolescence, but it long ago entered adulthood. (Cynics might even say that it's currently entering old age.) And, like our own, Montreal's special places have changed again and again over the three and one-half centuries of its existence. To the first inhabitants of this place everything was special — the land itself was sacred. Today, few Montrealers hold this view, but nearly every part of the city has a special significance for someone.

Montreal's most important landmark, and its most special place, is unquestionably Mount Royal. The mountain represents far more in emotional terms than one would expect from its looming, yet hardly overpowering presence. Almost every Montrealer has fond memories of walks, talks, picnics, winter games, summer sports, winter storms, and steamy summer

FIGURE 15

Snow-covered benches atop Mount-Royal

afternoons spent in Mount Royal Park. Because of the mountain's size (190 hectares) and central location, access to it is easy from much of the city. More than 150,000 people are able to walk to the park from their homes in fifteen minutes or less. Hike through the woods, bike up to a lookout, or feed the ducks on Beaver Lake: even a short outing can sooth many of the stresses and strains of everyday living.

From Mount Royal's highest lookout one can see most of the city's significant monuments. To the east, the Olympic Stadium dominates the skyline; to the south, one can see downtown and St. Helen's Island beyond it; to the north, the massive dome of St. Joseph's Oratory is visible; and to the west, Mies van der Rohe's triad of black skyscrapers, Westmount Square, jump out from their surroundings. But many more special places are hidden away in quiet and unremarkable corners of the city, sometimes unknown even to those who live near them.

Perhaps the most interesting recent addition to Montreal's pantheon of intriguing places is the Canadian Centre for Architecture. This extraordinary facility was built by Phyllis Lambert, an architect and heiress to the Bronfman family fortune. Lambert spared no expense in building a research and exhibition centre devoted to her lifetime passion. The CCA has amassed one of the largest existing collections of architectural documents, blueprints, photographs, and other material pertinent to the study of architecture. Some of the centre's original blueprints date back to medieval Europe. If you want to learn about the details of houses built in ancient Babylon, Confucian China, medieval Paris, or Depression-era St. Louis, the CCA is the place to go. No matter where you live or how small your house, the CCA probably has some information about the design of your bedroom!

The CCA is itself a celebration of architectural ingenuity, consisting in part of a lovingly restored turn-of-the-century mansion called Shaughnessy House. The ornately designed home was just one of dozens in the Golden Square Mile, as the area was known at the turn of the century. Shaughnessy House is one of the very few of those marvellous mansions to have escaped the wrecker's ball, and it has now been carefully

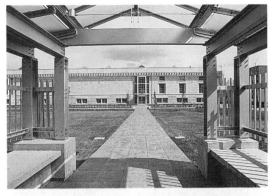

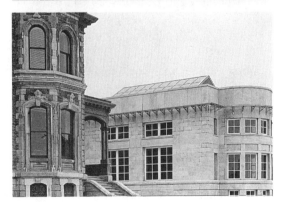

FIGURE 16

*Canadian Centre for Architecture
and the restored Shaughnessy House*

incorporated into a classically austere, yet distinctly modern U-shaped research centre. The CCA regularly presents touring exhibits, and draws as well on its own immense collections. Concerts are held in its exceptionally designed and crafted 225-seat auditorium, which is itself so peaceful and harmonious, so acoustically rich and well ventilated, that sitting in it for half an hour is almost like meditating in a cathedral.

On the edge of the escarpment that is situated across René Lévesque Boulevard from the CCA is an unusual park. Administered by the CCA and designed by Melvin Charney, the park is filled with freestanding architectural sculptures inspired by the buildings that characterize the neighbourhood that lies beneath the escarpment: St. Henri. Landscaped with rows of blooming apple trees, this half-moon-shaped park is surely one of the most pleasant spots in the city. When snow covers the cityscape below and a winter wind blows past, standing among the oddly majestic sculptures can be a unique experience.

On the other side of town, far to the east, another outdoor sanctuary may be found. While the Montreal Botanical Garden should be included on anyone's list of special places, there is, within the 73-hectare garden with its more than 26,000 species of plants, a particularly tranquil oasis. Le jardin du lac de rêve, or the Dream Lake Garden, was opened in 1991. The garden, intended to symbolize the harmonious intermingling of East and West, the friendship between China and Canada, was an entirely collaborative effort. Groves of Chinese bamboo alternate with Canadian maples. Naturally sculpted rocks from Shanghai's Lake Tai region are complemented by others quarried from Montreal's St. Helen's Island. The garden's seven traditional Chinese pavilions grace the Quebec landscape that contains them. Winding paths, stone bridges, a waterfall constructed of tons of hand-selected stones, meticulously arranged trees and flower beds, come together in this 2.5 hectare garden — the largest of its kind outside China — to create a magic atmosphere.

Across Sherbrooke Street from the gardens, yet worlds away, are a group of buildings that would undoubtedly have failed any test of architectural feasibility given by the experts at the CCA. The buildings in question are those built for the Montreal

FIGURE 17

The Olympic Stadium as seen from Mont-Royal Avenue

Olympics in 1976. The enormous circular stadium, commonly known as "The Big O," has become a symbol of incompetence, corruption, and profligacy to all Montrealers. Even the most cursory examination of the building's history would amaze anyone previously unfamiliar with it. For example, the stadium was intended to be the first with a retractable roof: the 26-ton roof, fabricated from the same material as bullet-proof vests, was designed to fold into the tilted tower from which it is suspended. This process, accomplished by means of a series of cables and winches, takes 45 minutes to complete. In 1987, 11 years behind schedule, the tower and roof were finally completed, but it turned out that the system wouldn't function properly. To make matters worse, the roofing material became damaged during storms — it could not withstand the elements. For this, Montreal taxpayers paid French architect Roger Taillibert 45 million dollars!

The stadium, which is home to the Montreal Expos, has been plagued by many other problems. Because the costs of its construction soared from 310 million to over 2 billion dollars, it is often referred to, only half-jokingly, as "The Big Owe." In 1991, a 55-ton chunk of concrete fell off the outside of the structure crushing a cluster of offices. The offices were, fortunately, empty at the time, but for a while some Montrealers refused to even enter the stadium.

For all its faults, however, the Olympic Stadium has often served its purpose well. With a seating capacity of 60,000, the enormous stadium, built in the shape of a mollusc, has inspired in Montrealers a certain grudging sense of pride. On occasion, the stadium is filled to capacity for concerts or sporting events; the cable-car ride up the tilted tower (the highest of its kind in the world) is another of the stadium's attractions. On a clear day, from the panoramic observatory on top of the tower, one can see for 80 kilometres.

Within the Olympic complex there are also exceptional aquatic facilities; the olympic-sized pools and diving towers are open to the public. The Velodrome, which was also located in the complex, was one of the finest public cycling facilities on the continent. However, in 1990, Mayor Jean Doré's administration decided to transform the Velodrome into a museum of the environment called the Biodome. While cyclists were upset by the destruction of the indoor cycling track, others lauded the idea of constructing a museum dedicated to educating citizens about the natural world. The Biodome opened in the late spring of 1992. To visit the museum is to escape to another world, or series of worlds, while remaining in the heart of the city. The Biodome is composed of re-creations of four distinct eco-systems: the Tropical Forest, the Laurentian Shield, the St. Lawrence Basin, and the Polar Sphere. As the visitor strolls through the transformed Velodrome, now lined with a wide variety of trees and flowers and populated with small animals and birds instead of speeding cyclists, the surrounding concrete jungle of the Olympic complex and the noisy urban sprawl beyond it seem increasingly remote.

In 1967, Montreal hosted a spectacular event: Expo 67, the world's fair. This massive exhibition, which was visited by over fifty million people, was held on a pair of islands situated in the St. Lawrence River facing the port of Montreal: St. Helen's Island and Île Nôtre Dame. In order to make room for the gigantic fair, St. Helen's Island was extended and Île Nôtre Dame was entirely created with landfill. The islands are now a public park, although sizeable sections of the decaying Expo 67 site have been fenced off. A large portion of St. Helen's Island has always been (and even was during the fair) a popular picnic spot; on summer weekends the lush green park is filled with Montrealers seeking relief from city heat and congestion. The eastern tip of St. Helen's Island is the site of an enormous amusement park called La Ronde, which was constructed for the world's fair and remains in operation today.

Expo 67 also inspired the construction of another important Montreal landmark: Habitat. This futuristic apartment build-ing, which appears from the distance to be a small mountain of randomly stacked boxes, was designed by architect Moshe Safdie as a model for low-cost housing units of the future. Habitat was visited by millions in 1967, and has now been fully occupied for more than two decades. The waiting list for an apartment there is nearly that long. Although Habitat is located in a rather remote and barren area of the city (at Cité du Havre facing Île Nôtre Dame), the apartments themselves are comfortable (and, ironically, expensive) and they offer stunning views of the river and the skyline of Montreal.

In recent times, it is events such as Expo 67, the 1976 Summer Olympics, and the Montreal International Jazz Festival that have drawn masses of people to the city. Yet it was not always so. During much of this century, tens of thousands of fervent Catholic pilgrims would make their way to Montreal each year to pray at St. Joseph's Oratory, one of the largest churches in the world. The oratory is an astoundingly large building. Its dome alone took 31 years to complete (from 1924 to 1955). Built into the face of the mountain above Queen Mary Road, the oratory completely dominates its environment. Not even the Olympic Stadium can match its imposing presence, although admittedly it comes close.

A tiny wooden shrine still stands beside the gargantuan oratory. Built in 1904 by Brother André, a monk belonging to the Society of the Brothers of the Holy Cross, the simple shrine became a symbol for Quebec's millions of Catholics. Despite, or perhaps because of, his illiteracy and humble character, Brother André was soon embraced as a healer and spiritual guide. He was credited with the miraculous healing of a number of his followers, and beatified by Pope John Paul II in 1982. After his death in 1937, Brother André was buried within the oratory. His heart was removed and placed on display for visitors. To compound the strangeness of the story, the heart was once stolen, causing an enormous outcry. The province was up in arms over this sacrilegious act, and thousands flocked to the oratory to pray for the heart's return. Within a few days, the heart was returned undamaged, and was promptly replaced in its display case. The episode is one of the more unusual in Montreal's history. To this day, half a million people visit the oratory annually, making it one of Montreal's most popular tourist attractions.

Let us now examine some of the city's more subtle points of interest. What many people enjoy most about visiting Montreal is not so much making the rounds of its main attractions as simply being out and about in the city itself. Montreal's vitality isn't limited to a few shopping plazas, museums, or important landmarks. What really makes Montreal exciting is its street

FIGURE 18

St. Joseph's Oratory

FIGURE 19

Cafés on St. Denis

life. Montreal is a city that makes an impression as a whole —
as a living entity, not as a loose collection of discrete sections.
Neighbourhoods flow into one another; commercial and residential buildings are interspersed in a way that eliminates
monotony.

If I had to take a visitor who had just arrived in the city on a
walk, I think I'd plan a leisurely afternoon stroll up St. Denis
Street. St. Denis is the axis of Montreal's nightlife, and of its
cultural life in general. Located in the centre of the city, the
street runs north-south, and, walking north from where it
intersects with Ste. Catherine Street — Montreal's primary
east-west commercial thoroughfare — it offers a host of fascinating distractions. Among the institutions to be found on the
next few blocks are the University of Quebec at Montreal, the
Cinémathèque Québécoise (a film archive and screening room),
the Théâtre St. Denis, and the National Library; there are, as
well, dozens of bars, nightclubs, cafés, first-class restaurants,
clothing stores, and boutiques displaying a tantalizing range of
merchandise. On weekend nights, St. Denis is jammed with
young and old, wealthy and not-so-wealthy, all heading to their
chosen destinations. Some proceed to the heavy-metal bars,
some to the pricey French restaurants, but only rarely can one
detect antagonism between the street's diverse visitors. St.
Denis belongs to all Quebecers, and all Quebecers know that.
In fact, on some nights it seems as though half of them have
congregated there.

No assessment of Montreal's special places could be complete
without at least mentioning the city's culinary delights. One
could list the French *pâtisseries*. One could also mention the
Greek, Italian, Spanish, Portuguese, Mexican, Latin American,
South American, Chinese, Japanese, Thai, Vietnamese, Eastern
European, Caribbean, and, of course, French restaurants. But
while Montrealers take pride in the great gastronomic diversity
their city's constantly changing restaurant scene provides, they
are at least as proud of two local specialties, those known
elsewhere in Canada as Montreal bagels and Montreal smoked
meat. These two simple delicacies can be found in abundance
on the Main and in the Plateau Mont Royal district. Two special
places, Schwartz's on the Main, famous for its smoked meat,

and the Bagel Shop on St. Viateur Street, renowned for its hot bagels that are available at any time of day or night, are well worth a visit (despite the line ups). While Montrealers in exile may pine for many of the things they left behind, nothing compares to their longing for bagels and smoked meat — you can tell by the dreamy look that appears in their eyes when these treats are mentioned. It may be the air, or the water, or the wood-burning stoves — who knows? — but there are no bagels like Montreal bagels, and that is a fact.

Finally, there is Old Montreal, first on the list of nearly all tourists. In North America, only Quebec City can offer a more breathtaking introduction to the buildings and monuments of centuries past than can Old Montreal. The district consists of the old port area, which is now primarily parkland and exhibition grounds, and the many blocks of old stone warehouses, private houses, stables, customs buildings, churches, and office buildings that surround it. Although few of the area's original edifices remain, most of the buildings in Old Montreal date back close to two hundred years. The district underwent a long period of revitalization that began in the early 1960s, and today, while it is full of the bustle of the tourist trade and of modern life in general, it still maintains a great deal of its Old World atmosphere. Place Jacques Cartier, in front of City Hall, is at the heart of the old quarter. It becomes a pedestrian mall in the summer when, on any given evening, it fills with sidewalk-café patrons, flower sellers, and street performers. But Old Montreal is not simply a tourist attraction or a place where locals come to relax; many businesses have established themselves here, including film-production companies, law offices, and high-end furniture stores. Some of the old stone warehouses have been converted into condominiums, and so a residential element has been reintroduced into an area that was once home to many Montrealers. Seeing how these contemporary businesses and dwellings have integrated themselves into the antique environment is half the fun of a walk through Old Montreal. Getting lost in the neighbourhood's maze of cobblestone streets is one of the definitive Montreal experiences.

SUGGESTED FURTHER READING

Choko, Marc H. *The Major Squares*. Trans. Käthe Roth. Montreal: Meridian, 1990.

A history of Montreal's Dorchester Square, Viger Square, Place D'Armes and Victoria Square showing the historical importance of large public spaces to the development of downtown Montreal.

Fraser, Matthew. *Quebec Inc.: French Canadian Entrepreneurs and the New Business Elite*. Toronto: Key Porter, 1987.

Gilmore, John. *Swinging in Paradise: The Story of Jazz in Montreal*. Montreal: Véhicule, 1988.

Gubbay, Aline. *Montreal: The Mountain and the River*. Trans. Rachel Levy. Montreal: Trillium, 1981.

A bilingual text tracing the history of Montreal from its founding to the present.

_____ . *A Street Called the Main: The History of Montreal's Saint-Laurent*. Montreal: Meridian, 1989.

Traces the history of Saint-Laurent from China Town to Jean-Talon Avenue.

Higgins, Benjamin. *The Rise and Fall of Montreal*. Moncton: Canadian Institute for Research on Regional Development, 1986.

A case study of urban growth, regional economic expansion and national development; a chronicle of Montreal's role, past and future, in the Canadian economy.

Irvin, Dick. *The Habs: An Oral History of the Montreal Canadiens, 1940–1980*. Toronto: McClelland, 1991.

Lazar, Barry and Tamsin Douglas. *The Guide to Ethnic Montreal*. Montreal: Véhicule, 1992.

A cultural guide to the city's neighbourhoods, restaurants, walking tours, clubs and organizations.

Mackay, Donald. *The Square Mile: Merchant Princes of Montreal*. Vancouver: Douglas and McIntyre, 1987.

A narrative and pictorial history of Montreal's "Golden Square Mile."

Marsan, Jean Claude. *Montreal in Evolution: An Historical Analysis of the Development of Montreal's Architecture and Urban Environment*. Montreal: McGill-Queens UP, 1990.

Follows the history of Montreal's architecture from the first settlement to the present.

Remillard, Francois, and Brian Merrett. *Montreal Architecture: A Guide to Styles and Buildings*. Trans. Pierre Miville-Deschenes. Montreal: Meridian, 1990.

An illustrated guide to the Architecture of Montreal showing the mingling of French and British traditions.

Rich, Edwin Ernest. *Montreal and the Fur Trade*. Montreal: McGill UP, 1966.

A history of Montreal's role in the North American fur trade.

Roy, Jean-Hugues, and Brendan Westson, eds. *Montreal: A Citizen's Guide to City Politics*. Montreal: Black Rose, 1990.

A critical analysis of the political scene in Montreal, covering issues urban planning and public housing to public health care and economic development. Includes essays by Montreal journalists, community activists, politicians and academics.

Sancton, Andrew. *Governing the Island of Montreal: Language Difference and Metropolitan Politics*. Berkeley: U of California P, 1985.

A study of biculturalism in Quebec.

Printed in Canada